THE
FORTUNATE ISLANDS

The Story of the Isles of Scilly

BY

E. L. BOWLEY

Published by W. P. KENNEDY,
ST. MARY'S, ISLES OF SCILLY, CORNWALL.

FIRST PUBLISHED 1945

SECOND EDITION 1947

THIRD EDITION 1949

Printed in Great Britain by

CROYDON TIMES LTD., HIGH STREET, CROYDON, SURREY

CONTENTS.

PAGE

Preface by the Secretary to the Duchy of Cornwall 4

Introduction 5

The Isles of the Blest 11

The Tin Islands 20

The Romans 41

Lyonesse 43

The Story of King Arthur 54

The Vikings and Saxons 62

From Athelstan to Queen Elizabeth 67

Star Castle 77

The Siege of Star Castle 94

The Scillionians 104

Local Customs 124

The Smith Dynasty 138

Robert Maybee 142

Wrecks, Wreckers and Smugglers 157

The Flower Industry 166

Bibliography 172

Index 175

PREFACE

(By Sir Clive Burn, K.C.V.O., Secretary and Keeper of the Records of the Duchy of Cornwall).

MUCH has been written from time to time on the subject of the Isles of Scilly, and in this book the Author has given us many interesting stories of the Islands and their inhabitants, both legendary and historical, which will be appreciated by those who know the Islands and are interested in their ancient history.

Mr. Bowley is to be congratulated on the amount of information he has collected, which must have occupied much time and laborious research.

To anyone contemplating a visit to these Islands this book will be of the greatest interest.

CLIVE BURN.

DUCHY OF CORNWALL OFFICE,
BUCKINGHAM GATE, S.W.1.

INTRODUCTION

STRABO, the Greek geographer, tells a story of a man, born in a small village called Aeolian Cyme, who wrote a history of the world in which he wished his birthplace to make a good contribution, but could not find that anything had ever happened there, so he ended each chapter:—" during all these stirring events Aeolian Cyme enjoyed profound tranquillity " !

The Isles of Scilly, though small and relatively insignificant in normal times, have been involved in many historical occasions, some of which have been peculiar and individual to them and have not affected the mainland, and others that have caused great and far-reaching effects on Great Britain and the Continent.

For several hundreds of years, learned men have disputed amongst themselves concerning what they have observed in the dim half-lights of the past. It is an absorbing pursuit to separate the legends from the myths and to satisfy oneself that the legends have not been wildly distorted from their factual bases. The stories of Scilly have been recorded mainly from external sources, by writers and poets none of whom could have had any bias in favour of extolling the virtues of the islands or of advancing their special historical claims to the attention of the public. It cannot be gainsaid that there is a very human tendency to acquire, for the benefit of one's own particular " Aeolian Cyme," merit for glories to which its claim is decidedly tenuous. In times gone by the monasteries, with their peculiar claims to sanctity based on legends, were not always above the reproach of importing stories rightfully belonging to other places.

I have attempted in this book to collate much of what has been said and written about the islands and to state a case for them wherever the title to their historical or archaeological patrimony has been assailed. I have endeavoured to restore to them their rightful claim to have been responsible for some highly colourful events which were in danger of being appropriated by other places less endowed with stories of their past.

This little archipelago lays claim to the title of the first centre of civilisation and culture in Northern Europe, where stone-age barbarians learnt the use of bronze and the arts of living from those Mediterranean seafarers who braved the "Pillars of Hercules," and made the Scillies their base in their search for gold, and later, for tin. It is claimed that the great Viking, Olaf Tryggvasson, was converted to Christianity while occupying the Islands and that as a direct result, the Christian religion was introduced to Norway, Sweden and Iceland. The Saga states that Olaf took with him from Scilly "priests and other learned men," which suggests that the Islands may have been a centre of secular as well as religious instruction.

The Islands were the rendezvous of the Spanish Armada, and later they defied the might of England under the Commonwealth, and the Dutch under the redoubtable Admiral Van Tromp, and maintained the flag of Charles I flying bravely from Star Castle, St. Mary's, five years after Parliament had assumed complete control of England. The Scilly Isles have the "distinction" of having received a "Declaration of War" from the Dutch, who were at the time at peace with England! They have the doubtful privilege of having been conquered by successive Vikings, by King Athelstan and by Admiral Blake, and in the course of centuries they have received Phœnicians, Iberians, Carthaginians, Belgic-Gauls, Celts, Danes, Turks, Moors (the pirates of Sallee), Vikings, Saxons, Romans and Britons; they have had their ups and downs of commerce—from the Isles of the Blest, where the chieftians of old were brought for eternal rest—they became the centre of commerce between the Mediterranean Countries and Ireland, the West of England and France; they developed an important shipbuilding industry in the days of wooden ships, and finally, in no whit disconcerted by changes of economic fortune, the shipwrights and sailors turned to flower farming, so that to-day nearly one hundred million blooms are supplied annually to the mainland markets.

Scilly can never be dissociated from its legends, and there is definitely something fey about the Islands which weave an enchanted spell over all those who visit them, and induce even in the sophisticated a state of mind inclined to give credence to the most fantastic tales, many of which must be classified in the cold light of calculated reason as myths.

Islands, as Conrad has remarked, are but the tops of mountains surrounded by an imponderable ocean, and the Scillies have been described elsewhere as the " hundred tops of a great mountain—emerging from the Deluge," and also as " a circular theatre or cluster of islands enclosing a land-locked sea of vivid blue." Mais describes the pond-like waters of Hugh Town harbour, St. Mary's, with the white sandy bottom of the shallow sea clearly visible, as " just the sort of place that Gulliver waded through to capture the fleet of Blefusco "; on the other hand, they were described in the time of Admiral Lord Seymour as "the strong and dangerous Isles of Scilly."

I have included a bibliography in the appendix, and I am especially indebted to the various writings of Messrs. J. E. Hooper, Lanje, E. J. Barth Ennor and F. McFarland (many of which have from time to time been published in the Islands' own Quarterly Magazine, "The Scillonian"), and to the recently published edition of the County Archæologies "Cornwall and Scilly," by H. O'Neill Hencken. The assistance of Mr. H. W. Kirk, sometime Keeper of the Records of the Duchy of Cornwall, is gratefully acknowledged; he has enabled me to include many hitherto unpublished records.

Finally, I desire to record my appreciation of the present Secretary of the Duchy of Cornwall Council, Sir Clive Burn, K.C.V.O., to whom I take leave to dedicate this book, and to Mr. T. M. Stanier, the Land Steward, both of whom have done so much for the Islanders in recent years.

E. L. BOWLEY.

1945.

STAR CASTLE,
ST. MARY'S,
ISLES OF SCILLY.

FOREWORD TO THE THIRD EDITION

In achieving its third edition within four years, " The Fortunate Islands " has demonstrated that an ever-growing number of people are interested in the Islands and desire to know something more about them than can be included in the guide-book. The opportunity has been taken to make some slight modifications in the text in the light of suggestions made to me since the second edition and, to those who have pointed out my omissions and queried some of my commissions, I am sincerely grateful.

E. L. B.

1949.

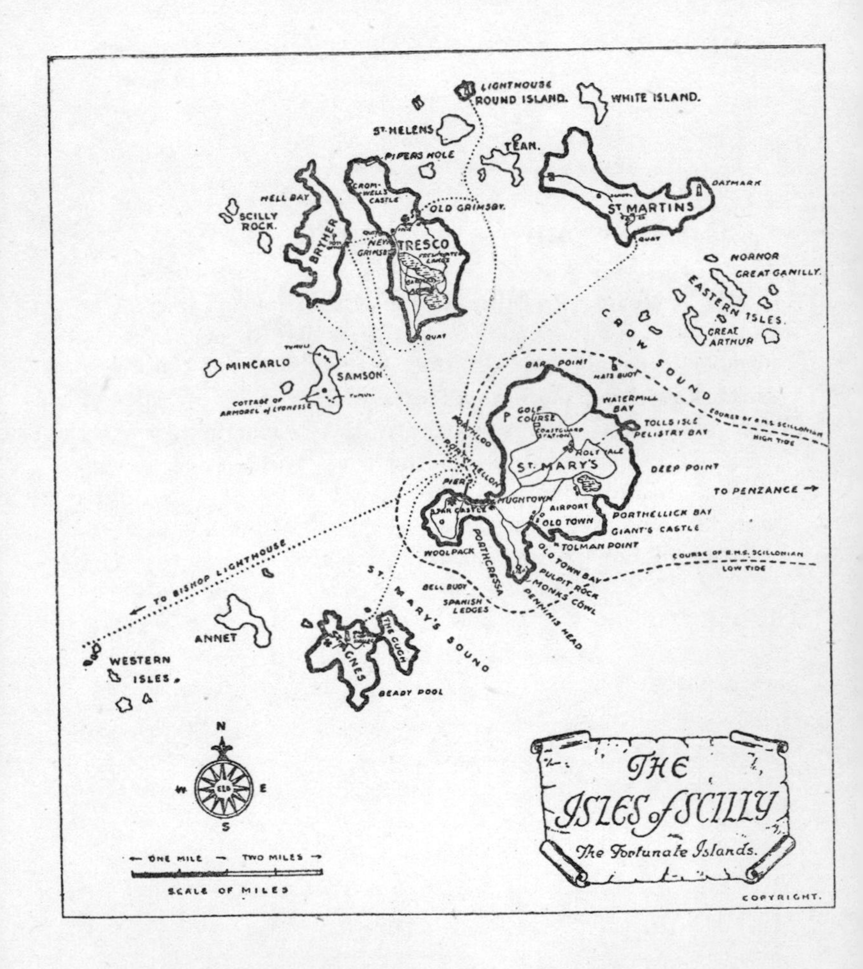
LIGHTHOUSE
ROUND ISLAND.
WHITE ISLAND.
ST. HELENS
TEAN.
PIPERS HOLE
ST MARTINS
HELL BAY
SCILLY ROCK.
BRYHER
OLD GRIMSBY.
TRESCO
NEW GRIMSBY
QUAY
NORNOR
GREAT GANILLY.
EASTERN ISLES.
GREAT ARTHUR
CROW SOUND
MINCARLO
SAMSON
BAR POINT
WATERMILL BAY
GOLF COURSE
TOLLS ISLE
PELISTRY BAY
ST. MARY'S
DEEP POINT
TO PENZANCE
PIER
HUGHTOWN
AIRPORT
PORTHELLICK BAY
OLD TOWN
GIANT'S CASTLE
TOLMAN POINT
WOOLPACK
PORTHCRESSA
OLD TOWN BAY
PULPIT ROCK
MONKS COWL
PENNINIS HEAD
TO BISHOP LIGHTHOUSE
BELL BUOY
SPANISH LEDGES
ST. MARY'S SOUND
ANNET
WESTERN ISLES
AGNES
THE GUGH
BEADY POOL
N
W
E
S
ONE MILE
TWO MILES
SCALE OF MILES
THE ISLES of SCILLY
The Fortunate Islands.
COPYRIGHT.

THE ISLES OF THE BLEST

" What shall we tell you? Tales, marvellous tales
Of ships and Stars and Isles where good men rest,
Where nevermore the rose of sunset pales,
And winds and shadows fall towards the West."

(JAMES ELROY FLECKER.)

THE legends and folk-lore concerning the " Isles of the Blest," or " Fortunate Islands," originated from the Celtic family of nations and referred to a land of the Dead situated to the west on an island, or islands, in the Atlantic Ocean. The Celts called the island " Avalon," or " Glasinnis," and told wondrous tales of it with all the wealth of fancy and imagination for which they are noted. Mediæval manuscripts contain many references to mysterious islands where heroes find immortality and a never-ending round of pleasures amidst perpetual summer and abundance—the " happy islands of the heroic dead." They refer frequently to the " Land of Shades " in Western or South-Western Britain and some tell of islands where peculiar sacrifies were performed, of islands forbidden to men and occupied by women, and of islands inhabited solely by holy men.

Stories of islands to the West of the known world were frequently mentioned in Greek and Latin mythology. The islands were placed beyond the " Pillars of Hercules " (Straits of Gibraltar) and they were variously called the " Fortunatæ Insulæ," " The Islands of the Blest," " The Hesperides," " The Elysian Fields " or " Atlantis."

The inhabitants of these islands dwelt in beautiful meadows, rich with flowers and sunshine which never failed, where they disported themselves with music and games. It was believed that its rulers invaded Europe but were repulsed by the Athenians. Subsequently the ocean swallowed them up on account of the profligacy of their inhabitants.

They are mentioned in the works of Plato, Pliny, Diodorus and others and were usually regarded as reserved for the elect and the heroes of unusual prowess who were translated to these fabled islands without dying.

We have spoken of these islands as imaginary or mythical, but they may have had a real existence, and if so, there are several claimants to the title. The first, which is the most interesting, was propounded by one Bircherod, in a treatise " De Orbe Novo non Novo " (1685), who maintained that Phœnician or Carthaginian trading ships, driven by storm, had *reached the American coast*, and had returned thence bringing with them marvellous tales of the New World, which formed the basis of the widespread belief in an Atlantis!

In the Tertiery period, long, long before any scrap of tradition could possibly have commenced, France was joined to America, and there was a very large island continent to the west of Spain; the Canaries are believed to represent all that is left of this continent and are sometimes referred to as " Atlantis " and, for this reason also, they are sometimes referred to as " The Fortunate Islands." The Canaries were known by repute to the geographers of Greece and Rome, but for many centuries lost sight of, they were not rediscovered until 1334.

The claim of the Scillies to the title of " The Fortunate Islands " rests on the Celtic origin of the story, and on the evidence of the barrows and sepulchral remains on the Islands which, according to the archæologist, H. O'Neill Hencken, possess three times as many chambered barrows of the Megalithic period as exist upon the whole of Cornwall, a county that is itself noted for them. These barrows are out of all proportion to the number and style of the persons who, according to the evidence of excavated

Photo : King, Scilly.

Garrison Gateway, St. Mary's.

St. Mary's Pool and Star Castle. *Photo : Gibson, Scilly.*

villages, were then natives of the Islands, and there is every reason to believe that the graves were erected as a permanent resting place for princes and leaders of far greater renown than could have been gained or supported locally.

It is probable that lonely islands were invested with a peculiar sanctity for reasons of safety; in prehistoric times there could have been little security on large tracts of land which were liable to raids, whereas islands, owing to their inaccessibility, provided the obvious depository for sentimental and material treasures and also presented an opportunity for the steady progress of culture and the arts. There may have been a belief that the spirits of the departed could not travel across water, and would not therefore return to cause embarrassment to their successors.

There can be little doubt of the existence of a Celtic tradition of a Land of the Dead on islands to the west of Britain.

Hencken suggests that the Scillies may have been the isles off Western Britain referred to by Plutarch as follows:

" . . . . Demetrius further said, that of the islands around Britain many be scattered about uninhabited, of which some are named after deities and heroes. He told us also, that, being sent by the emperor with the object of reconnoitring and inspecting, he went to the island which lay nearest to those uninhabited, and found it occupied by few inhabitants who were, however, sacrosanct and inviolable in the eyes of the Britons.

" Soon after his arrival a great disturbance of the atmosphere took place, accompanied by many portents, by the winds bursting forth into hurricanes and by fiery bolts falling. When it was over, the islanders said that some of the mighty had passed away. For, as a lamp on being lit, they said, brings with it no danger, while on being extinguished it is grievous to many, just so with regard to great souls, their beginning to shine forth is pleasant and the reverse of grievous, whereas the extinction and destruction of them frequently disturb the winds and the surge as at present; also do they infect the atmosphere with the pestilential diseases. Moreover, there is there, they said, an island in which Cronus is imprisoned, with Briareus keeping guard over him as he sleeps; for, as they put it, sleep is the bond forged for Cronus. They add that around him are many deities, his henchmen and attendants."

In the 18th Century, Dr. Borlase, while excavating one of the barrows, was interrupted by a similar storm and was warned by the natives that it was a sign of the wrath of the giants, caused by his impious labours.

Plutarch tells of four islands that lie to the west of Britain in one of which Zeus had imprisoned the Irish chieftain Kronos in a deep cave, and fettered him with sleep by the music of a magic harp, and where he is ministered by spirits in the form of birds; the island is a "pleasant place where there is an abundance of good things." Irish divinities frequently assumed the form of birds.

According to Procopius: "Along the continental shore were villages of mariners, some of whom every night ferried over the dead; at the shore were strange ships, not their own, which they manned, and though the seamen saw no one, the vessels sank to the gunwales under the weight of invisible passengers and then suddenly, with magic speed, they reached the distant island; on arrival the boats lightened, though the seamen see no one, but only hear a Voice calling over the names and dignities and hereditary titles of those who have crossed and, being thus released from that which they have been constrained to do, the seamen immediately return."

The story of the Scillies would not be complete without some reference to their many prehistoric remains and to the theories connected with them, and it is inevitable that any history should commence with the evidence provided by tombs and sepulchral monuments and lead up, in the case of these Islands, to the riot of flowers of the present day.

Barrows and their contents tell a story, a story of changes in religious thought through the Ages. From the days of Egypt's greatness, the idea of the survival of the body and the practice of preserving it, has grown or diminished according to the particular religious ideas of the time; the Egyptians discovered the art of mummifying their dead, which entailed a tomb, hence the Pyramids and vaults of varying degree, but when the concept of the survival of the spirit only became prevalent, the Egyptians, who had lost the art of embalming, still used the vaults for the cremated ashes of the departed. As Mr. John Layard has pointed out, this curious anomaly of building an everlasting vault for the reception of nothing more than mortal ashes, has persisted throughout the ages. The spread of religious ideas from Egypt and the East is well demonstrated in the Scilly Islands, where all these burial methods are represented.

The earliest known trace of human activity on the Scillies has been discovered in a barrow on The Gugh, St. Agnes, in which, below the cremated remains of Middle Bronze Age people (who adopted cremation), bones were found indicating an earlier period when inhumation was practised. Inhumation (the practice of burying the complete body first of all in the contracted position and, at a later date, in the extended position) existed until about 1700 B.C., when cremation became common and urns were placed upside down in already existing barrows; from about 600 B.C., the construction of barrows was discontinued and urnfields became the rule. In addition to passage-graves and covered galleries, numerous cists or stone boxes, usually made of four stones set at right-angles and covered by a single cap stone, are still to be seen on the different islands; there are four monoliths, or standing-stones, the purport of which, it is surmised, was connected with Early Bronze Age Ceremonial. Similar monoliths are found in Syria, Egypt and Brittany. Pottery and funeral urns, stone mace-heads and flint instruments, holed stones, saddle querns and stone mortars, frequently come to light to prove that the islands were inhabited at least as early as 4,000 years ago. There is also the evidence of the ruins of several small, round prehistoric huts, and the contents of the surrounding middens, or refuse dumps. A comparison of these insignificant huts with the massive masonry of the tombs shows that vastly more importance was attached to the abodes of the dead, whether natives or not, than to those of the living. Unfortunately, for archæologists, the main barrows have been despoiled and the contents scattered to the four winds.

The barrows, with their enormous blocks of solid granite, demonstrate a high degree of engineering skill; we do not know how they were installed with primitive instruments, but splitting was achieved by means of dry wooden wedges inserted at intervals, and soaked with water until the expansion of the wood split the whole boulder. Many blocks seen on the islands still show the indentations caused by the holes made for the wedges. Dr. Borlase, the Cornish antiquarian, declared that many of the rock basins and conformations on Scilly are unmistakably connected with the ceremonies of the Druids, who for some thousand years B.C. represented the only co-ordinated control over the different tribes in the British Isles: so-called sacrificial altars and stones, holed and otherwise, connected with the pagan worship of the sun, may abound, but the subject is highly controversial and, because of the weird effects of wind and weather on granite, it will never be possible to state definitely on which of these stones the hand of man has intervened. Historians and archæologists of the present day do not profess to know nearly as much about the Druids as did those who wrote about them in previous generations! It can nevertheless be assumed that before the days of parchment and written contracts, ceremonies were undergone at fixed places (as witness the hole stones through which bride and groom clasped hands to plight their troth) and some of which were reserved for the punishment of criminals or those who had offended the established power.

Timæus, writing of the " Islands in the Ocean," states: " Opposite to Celtiberia are a number of islands, by the Greeks called Cassiterides, in consequence of their abounding in tin; and facing the promontory of the Arrotrebæ, are the six islands of the gods, which some persons have called the Fortunate Islands."

" Opposite to " infers a location at right angles to the line of coast, and the Scillies are at right angles to the long northern coast of Spain. It may be assumed, therefore, that Timæus failed to associate the promontory with Celtiberia, and thus gave a different location to the Tin and Fortunate Islands.

Pliny says that " over against Celtiberia are very many Isles called by the Greeks Cassiterides for the plenty of lead (tin) they yield; and just against the promontory of the Arrotrebæ, six named Deorum (of the Gods) which some have called Fortunatæ."

On the subject of the promontory of the Arrotrebæ, Pliny asserts that the Fortunate Islands are " just against it," and adds that " On the one hand is the North and the Gaul's Ocean, on the other, the West and the Atlantic Ocean."

The world beyond the Straits of Gibraltar was a very dim world indeed to the early historians, mainly because the Phœnicians controlled the Straits and kept their trade secrets, the chief of which was the source of tin.

THE TIN ISLANDS.

THERE can hardly be a more absorbing pursuit than to examine the earliest records relating to "Homo Sapiens" and endeavour to separate the myths, which are stories without foundation, from the legends, which have a basis of fact albeit embellished by the story-tellers of successive generations. We have to strip the legend of its decorations and draw inferences as to what really did happen. As an example there is the legend of the Tyrian Hercules, the merchant and navigator King of Tyre, from some of whose exploits the labours of the Grecian Hercules were appropriated: our Tyrian Hercules invaded Iberia (which was later colonised) probably first at Tartessus, and later still at Gades, and in the course of his visit he is related to have fought the giant Geryon who had three heads or three bodies, which statement has been explained as indicating that he fought three native princes who were allied against him. One of his labours represents a descent into Hades, and may have indicated that he visited the land of shades—or "beyond the known world."

Wherever written records are lacking and archæological survivals scarce or inconclusive, we must fall back upon the "clamorous voice of tradition," which at one time was discredited, but the discoveries of the last half century in the Middle East have caused, amongst historians, a profound change of view, and tradition, shorn of supernatural trappings, has been rehabilitated; of the traditions no longer suspect as myths or figments of the imagination, we can safely place the Trojan war and many figures of the heroic age, including Hercules of Tyre.

The Ancients had no satisfactory way of commemorating the exploits of great heroes other than to allot to them a place in the hierarchy of their divinities, and to perpetuate their memory by legends connected with their outstanding feats. Some of the legends of the Phœnicians, and later of the Greeks, have a place in the story of the Isles of Scilly, as they provide evidence both for and against the conjecture that the Scillies were the Cassiterides of the Phœnicians and the Hesperides of the Greeks.

This question has been the cause of an immense amount of disputation amongst the learned men, from the time of recorded history down to the present day, and we have no doubt that there is not enough evidence to justify the dogmatic asseverations that have been made on either side. The reader will draw his own conclusions on the theory that is advanced here, that the Islands were the first to supply tin to the Mediterranean, and that later they formed the entrepôt or trading centre for Cornish tin until, in more settled times, Mount St. Michael in Cornwall acquired the trade.

It is an intriguing story ranging from Devonshire cream to the Trojan War, and literally from China to Peru, and commences somewhere in the period of world history dating from B.C. 1500 to the "Pax Romana" in Gaul (about B.C. 50).

All these events occurred so long ago that our imagination can only with difficulty appreciate the fact that it covers a period of human activity equal to that from today to the Dark Ages, when King Arthur was credited with his great battles with the invading Saxons. We must therefore make some slight reference to dates, for we cover a vast stretch of time, and they are the sole means of establishing any kind of continuity to our story. We must in addition sketch in some part of the background—and what a magnificent background it is—which leads us unerringly to the great cities of Sidon and Tyre which were situated on the eastern shores of the Mediterranean, and from whence, we contend, came our first visitors. They brought salt, earthenware vessels and brass, sought gold, and later tin, which metal their artificers used for making bronze utensils and for distilling the famous purple dye, and even for the manufacture of ladies' hand-mirrors of a shape not unlike those in use today. One would hesitate to say that these visitors brought us our first introduction to civilisation, since our natives of 1500 B.C. erected their permanent monuments and were undoubtedly organised, in later times, under the Druidical system.

Our story is written within the confines of a few small rocks, and it may be that their insignificant size and the fact that they existed for so many ages, and that so much has happened on them, acts as a stimulus to our imagination and invests the granite with an aura demanding a quite unnecessary degree of veneration. On the other hand, it is not of rocks that we are concerned but of their use under the hand of our ancestors, and most of us are influenced consciously or otherwise, by our traditions: our own certainty about our beliefs may well blind us to any weakness in the arguments we use to support them!

What sort of people were these Phœnicians? They were firstly traders and artificers, then navigators, and, by necessity, colonists. They lived on a narrow strip of land we now call Syria, had few agricultural opportunities and were unique in those times in having no apparent political ambitions. Sidon was the parent, and later, Tyre, whose merchants established colonies on all the Mediterranean shores, notably Carthage, and beyond the inland sea at Gades, from whence they continued the process along the shores of Africa southwards, and Spain and Gaul northwards and, we believe, even beyond Gaul.

For generations they had complete maritime supremacy; they navigated by the sun, moon and pole star, and, probably in the cause of trade, were inquisitive and venturesome; they organised the then known world for their own requirements but did not spread their culture to subject races, or customers, in the manner of the Greeks and Romans after them.

Ezekiel (*circa* 600 B.C.) in the following magnificent description speaks of the Phœnicians and their ships: "Thy borders are in the midst of the seas, thy builders have perfected thy beauty. They have made all thy ship boards of fir-trees of Senir; they have taken Cedars from Lebanon to make masts for thee. Of the oaks of Bashan have they made thine oars; the company of the Ashurites have made thy benches, of ivory brought out of the isles of Chittim. Fine linen with broidered work from Egypt was that which thou spreadest forth to be thy sail; blue and purple from the isles of Elishah was that which covered thee. The inhabitants of Zidon and Arvad were thy mariners; thy wise men, O Tyrus, that were in thee, were thy pilots. The Ancients of Gebal and the wise men thereof were, in thee, thy calkers: all the ships of the sea with their mariners were in thee to occupy thy merchandise . . . . Tarshish was thy merchant by reason of the multitude of all kinds of riches; with silver, iron, tin and lead they traded in thy fairs . . . many isles were the merchandise of thine hand . . . ."

In the Oeconomicus of Xenophon, a Greek is represented as saying: " The best and most accurate arrangement of things, I think, that I ever saw, was when I went to look at the great Phœnician ship. For I saw the greatest quantity of tackling separately disposed in the smallest storage. You know that a ship comes to anchor or gets under way by means of many wooden instruments, and many ropes, and sails by means of many sails, and is armed with many machines against hostile vessels, and carries about with it many arms for the crew, and all the apparatus which men use in a dwelling house, for each mess. Besides all this, the vessel is filled with cargo which the owner carries for profit. And all that I have mentioned lay in not much greater space than would be found in a chamber large enough for ten beds. All things, too, lay in such a way that they did not obstruct one another, so that they needed no one to seek them, could be easily got together, and there were no knots to be untied, and cause delay, if they were suddenly wanted for use."

Shipshape and Bristol (or Phœnician) fashion!

Their captains or navigators were worthy of their ships. Herodotus states that in 600 B.C.—two thousand years before Vasquez da Gama's voyage of discovery round the Cape of Good Hope—the Phœnicians, starting from the Red Sea, circumnavigated Africa! Strabo states that they sailed "beyond the Mediterranean" very soon after the Trojan War (*circa* 1200 B.C.). The Phœnician colony of Gades (Cadiz) was founded, according to the authorities, at about this period, and we can therefore make a strong presumption that they voyaged northwards also; in fact, it is unlikely that they would have established a colony and trading centre at the extreme perimeter of their explorations. They established a fishery for conger-eels and tunny (we learn from Kenrickes' "Phœnicia") four days' sail in the waters of the Atlantic, and even supplied the fish market in Jerusalem.

What an epic could be written on the voyage of Melkarth, the Tyrian "Hercules," navigating beyond the known world to the "Shades," over the edge of the earth, and eventually finding the Cassiterides and tin! Alas, we have so little record, and what we have was written many generations after the event. All we have are the legends and the statement of Diodorus Siculus that, after having reduced Spain to order, Hercules proceeded northward through Celtica, putting " an end to the usual impieties and murdering of strangers," founded Arras and fought the giants Albion (!) and Bergion. Pliny states that " Midacritus (the Greek name for Melkarth) was the first who brought tin from the island called Cassiteris."

One fact that clearly emerges is that the Phœnicians and their successors of Carthage were colonists. The Periplus of Scylax states: " from the Pillars of Hercules on the European coast there lay many settlements of the Carthaginians." Not only did they colonise the islands and shores of the Mediterranean, but Carthage is known to have equipped and despatched two colonising expeditions, one, under Hanno, through the Straits of Gibraltar southwards along the West Coast of Africa, and one under Hamilco (brother of Hanno) to Gaul and Britain, where they found the tin market. Hanno is known to have established six cities, and Hamilco, though the records are lost, is reputed to have been equally successful. Each expedition comprised 30,000 colonists, men, women and children, with sixty vessels. The date of these expeditions is unknown, but some authorities place it at 450 B.C. We have confirmation of this expedition from Festus Avienus, who, in a poem, " Ora Maritima," relates:—

" Where the ocean flood presses in, and spreads wide the Mediterranean waters, lies the Atlantic Bay; here stands Gadira, of old Tartessus, here the Pillars of Hercules, Abyla, left of Iibya, and Calpe . . . (missing record) . . . Here rises the head of the promontory in olden times named Oestrymnon; and below the like-named bay and isles; wide they stretch, and are rich in metals, tin and lead. There a numerous race of men dwell, endowed with spirit, and no slight industry, busied all in the cares of trade alone. They navigate the sea on their barks, built not of pines or oaks, but, wondrous! made of skins and leather.

" Two days long is the voyage thence to the Holy Island, once so called, which lies expanded on the sea, the dwelling of the Hibernian race, at hand lies the isle of Albion.

" Of yore the trading voyages from Tartessus reached to the Oestrymnides, but the Carthaginians and their colonies near the Pillars of Hercules, navigated in this sea, which Hamilco, by his own account, was upon during four months."

Some authorities claim that the Oestrymnides were the Western Islands off Brittany, but, although those Islands may well have been a port of call, they are not known to have possessed any native tin; moreover, they are more than " two days' sail " to Hibernia (Ireland) and cannot be described as being " at hand " to Albion.

The Phœnicians did not leave any monuments or material tokens by which their occupation could be fixed for future reference, and this applies not only to the colonies outside the Mediterranean, but to those within that sea and even close to Tyre, such as Cyprus, Crete and Sicily. Hencken, in commenting on the scarcity of archæological *cultural* finds in the extreme West, suggests that owing to the dense population and the scarcity of agricultural land, the tin miners may have purchased food and other perishable necessities in exchange for their tin; they may well have traded the implements of brass and ornaments (mentioned by several ancient writers) in exchange for food from the agricultural areas of Britain. There are, nevertheless, some slight indications which, if they cannot be accepted as evidence of Phœnician occupation, are at least curious: Devonshire cream, which was at one time confined to Cornwall and Devon west of the River Exe, is said to be known in one other part of the world only, namely in Syria. Was the art of making this delicacy " melt-in-the-mouthy Cornish cream " which, as the poet has it, is " of the colour of buttercups newly born," brought over by the Phœnicians from Tyre?

A custom prevailed in Scilly and West Cornwall until recently of addressing persons of middle rank by the appellation "Uncle" or "Aunt," not only by children, but by adults, and as a form of respect rather than familiarity—this is said to be a custom existing still in Andalusia, which is known to have been colonised by the Phœnicians. "On Shrove Tuesday, the boys of this island" (St. Mary's) says Heath (1750) "have a custom of throwing stones in the evening against the doors of the dwellers' houses, a privilege they claim from time immemorial;" he was informed "that the same custom is still used in several Provinces of Spain."

There is also a curious similarity between the emblems on some of the Cornish crosses and an emblem displayed on some early coins of the Ægean region. In an article by Chas. A. Eva in the "Old Cornwall" Magazine, it is pointed out that Market Crosses and pillars were erected by the Greeks as a symbol of Hermes, the god of merchandise; he suggests that the form of these pillars survived in the pagan merchant crosses, of much later date, in Cornwall and the West of England.

STATER, 600 B.C. OBOL, 550 B.C.
COINS from ÆGEAN ISLES.

Dionysius Alexandrius describes the Island as follows:

"Against the sacred Cape* great Europe's head,
Th' Hesperides along the ocean spread:
Whose wealthy hills with mines of tin abound,
And stout Iberians till the fertile ground."

Tin was definitely in use at Sidon and Tyre before the Trojan War. There is a reference in Genesis, shortly after the description of the flood, to Tubal Cain "an instructor of every artificer in brass" (the "brass" of the Old Testament was probably "bronze"). It was found among the spoils of the Midianites (*circa* 1400 B.C.) in the days of Moses. Ezekiel speaks of Tyre as having long been the emporium "for many Isles," and of "Tarshish" he says: "O thou that art situate at the entry of the sea, which art a merchant of the people of many Isles . . ." There are numerous references to tin as one of the main articles of Phœnician commerce; since they were primarily traders, they succeeded in keeping the source of the tin secret for at least 500 years. The mystery was so well preserved that Julius Cæsar when he landed in Britain was not aware that he had come to the land "whence tin came," although the helmets, shields, and breastplates of his centurions were composed of some ten per cent. of the metal, originating from Cornwall. The secret must have been known to the Phocean Greeks who founded Marseilles (Massilia) *circa* 600 B.C. Posidonius states that the tin was brought in 320 B.C. to Massilia and that the Massilians were the first to break the Phœnician monopoly. Strabo (*circa* A.D. 18) relates: "Formerly, the Phœnicians alone carried on this traffic (tin) from Gades, concealing the passage from everyone, and when the Romans followed a certain ship master that they also might find the market, the ship master, of jealousy, purposely ran his vessel upon a shoal, leading on

*Ortegal.

those who followed him into the same destructive disaster; he himself escaped by means of a fragment of the ship, and received from the Public Treasury the value of the ship and cargo he had lost. The Romans, nevertheless, by frequent efforts, discovered the passage." This " jealousy " is sufficient to explain, in part, the veil of mystery that shrouded the early source of tin, and it is necessary to add that the traders may have encouraged the idea that the commodity was to be found on islands which, by their nature, would be all the more difficult for their rivals to discover.

The problem that we have to unravel is, from whence did the Ancients bring their tin into the great marts at Gades, Carthage and Tyre? Is it reasonable to assume that they found it in Northern Europe at all, and, if so, did it come first from Scilly and later from West Cornwall, via Scilly, and finally direct from West Cornwall? We have shown that the Phœnicians could and did navigate their ships enormous distances, that they were venturecome and unlikely to miss a satisfactory supply of a commodity in which they specialised and maintained a monopoly, and we have good reason for assuming that they did not obtain the metal from Spain, which source could hardly have been kept secret and which is not known to have produced any quantity of tin in historical times. There is no other satisfactory source known in Europe. Pliny says: " It (tin) is extracted with great labour in Spain and throughout all the Gallic provinces, but in Britannia it is found in the upper stratum of the earth in such abundance, that a law has been spontaneously made prohibiting anyone from working more than a certain quantity of it."

India, which has tin in abundance, must be considered; the Chinese bronze age, 1800 B.C.—1500 B.C., was even more ancient than that of which we write and it is probable that some Indian tin was sent to China, but, apart from the fact that the voyage from the Mediterranean to India was more than twice the distance to Britain, we have it on authority that India imported tin from the Mediterranean in exchange for spices and other commodities. We know that " Tarshish was thy ' merchant,' " and, although there may have been many places named Tarshish, none has ever been suggested on the Indian route via the Red Sea. Tarshish was probably Tartessus, on the Western coast of Spain. Some weight must be given, we think, to the fact that the earliest writers (who were nearest to the period concerned and were in the best position to study records now lost to us and to listen to and compare the legends that were current) are unanimous in maintaining that the source was beyond the Pillars of Hercules (the Straits of Gibraltar). The descriptions tend in many cases towards Britain, and some go into detail and specify islands, and a few give descriptions which are not to be lightly dismissed, as referring to the Scillies. They lack definition, but some have, nevertheless, circumstantial detail not usually associated with wild guesswork.

Herodotus, the first Greek historian, who wrote in 450 B.C., and whose writings go back to a period 250 years before his time, says: " of that part of Europe nearest to the West, I am not able to speak with decision. I by no means believe that the barbarians give the name of Eridanus to a river which empties itself into the Northern Sea; whence, it is said, our amber comes. Neither am I better acquainted with the islands called the Cassiterides, from which we are said to have our tin . . . . It is, nevertheless, certain that both our tin and our amber are brought from these extreme regions." This statement is exceptionally interesting, since it places the source of the tin at an " extreme " distance, comparable with the source of amber in the Baltic, and thus eliminates Spanish tin from the concept of Herodotus. Eridanus is probably the Rhodane river near Danzig, where amber is even now obtained in large quantities. Plutarch mentioned that it was said that gold came from the North of Europe and was obtained from the Arimaspians, a one-eyed people, who steal it from the Griffons! Aristotle, writing about a century later than Herodotus, reveals that the geographical knowledge of the Greeks was very limited:—" Beyond the Pillars of Hercules, the ocean flows around the earth: in this ocean, however, are two islands, those very large, called Britannia; Albion and Ierne, which are larger than those before mentioned, and lie beyond the Kelti; and another two not less than these—Taprobane, beyond the Indians, lying obliquely in respect of the main land, and that called Phebol, situate over against the Arabic Gulf; moreover, not a few small islands, around the Britannic Isles and Iberia, encircle as with a diadem this earth, which we have already said to be an island."

Strabo (A.D. 18) says: " The Cassiterides, opposite to the West Parts of Britain, situate as it were in the same climate with Britain, are ten in number and lie near each other in the ocean toward the North from the haven of the Artabri. One of them is desert, but the others are inhabited by men in black cloaks, clad in tunics reaching to the feet, girt about the breast, and walking with staves, thus resembling the furies we see in tragic representations. They subsist by their cattle, leading for the most part a wandering life. Of the metals, they have tin and lead, which, with skins, they barter with the merchants for earthenware, salt and brazen vessels." George Smith, in " The Cassiterides," quotes this account by Tacitus regarding the Roman invasion of Anglesey: " Women were seen rushing through the ranks in wild disorder, their apparel funereal, their hair loose in the wind, in their hands flaming torches, and their whole appearance resembling the frantic rage of furies. The Druids were ranged in order, with hands uplifted, invoking the gods and pouring forth horrible imprecations. The novelty of the sight struck the Romans with awe and terror. They stood in stupid amazement, as if their limbs were benumbed, riveted to one spot, a mark for the enemy." The earliest British " Secret Weapon "!

After the great period of megalithic culture, the inhabitants of Britain deteriorated, and it was said of the Britons in Caesar's time that " only the inhabitants of the Southern coast covered their nakedness with the skins of beasts, and this rather to avoid giving offence to the strangers who came to trade with them than out of any principle of decency! "

Solinus states tht the Tin Islands were " severed from the coast of Damnonii by a rough narrow sea." The Damnonii were occupants of Devon and Cornwall long before the South-Western part was named Cornubia, and no trace of them can be found elsewhere until they colonised Armorica (Brittany) in the fifth century. Solinus further refers to the Tin Islands:

" Oft the Tartessians thro' the well-known seas,
Wou'd sail for Traffic to the Oestrymnides;
And Carthagians, too . . . ."

Pliny says " opposite to Celtiberia are a number of islands, by the Greeks called Cassiterides, in consequence of their abounding in tin." Pliny mentions " Mictis, an island about six days' sail inward* from Britain, said to be fertile in tin, and to this island the Britons came in boats of osier covered with sewn hides." He may have been referring to St. Michael's Mount or the Scillies, since, as Borlaze remarks: " the Ancients reckoned days of sail not from the nearest place, but from the place most known and

*i e., towards the Mediterranean.

frequented by them (Romans and Gauls) which was that part of Britain nearest to, and within sight of, Gaul—a reasonable six days' sailing distance to the Islands." The Romans were not the equivalent of the Phoenicians as navigators, and would have brought their ships along the coast to connect with the overland traffic coming to the Gallic coast opposite to the Isle of Wight or Dover. They may not have ventured the direct crossing from Ushant. Antonius mentions an island called Lissia—which may have been the Wolf Rock. The following is the account of Diodorus Siculus, who lived in the first century B.C., which has been translated by W. Ridgeway as follows:—

"The inhabitants of that part of Britain which is called Balerium (Land's End) are very fond of strangers, and from their intercourse with foreign merchants, are civilised in their manner of life. They prepare the tin, working very carefully the earth in which it is produced. The ground is rocky, but it contains earthy veins, the produce of which is ground down, smelted and purified. They beat the metal into masses shaped like astragali (dice) and carry it to a certain island lying off Britain called Ictis (St. Michael's Mount). During the ebb of the tide the intervening space is left dry and they carry over into this island the tin in abundance in their waggons. Now there is a peculiar phenomenon connected with the neighbouring islands, I mean those that lie between Europe and Britain, for at the flood tide the intervening passage is overflowed, and they seem like islands, but a large space is left dry at the ebb and they seem to be like peninsulars. Here then the merchants buy the tin from the natives and carry it over to Gaul and, after travelling overland for about thirty days, they finally bring their loads on horses to the mouth of the Rhone. Thus much concerning tin." Ictis is generally accepted as applying to St. Michael's Mount, Cornwall, and it should be remembered that Diodorus was writing of the

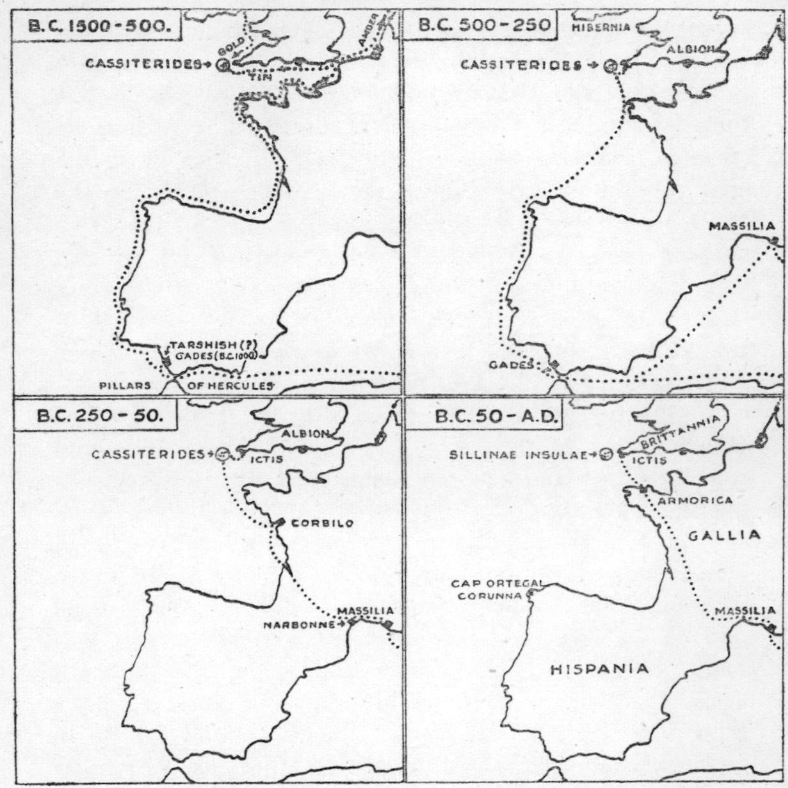

The transport of tin by sea and land through the centuries.

---

traffic in his time, and after Gaul had been brought under control by the Romans. The port in Gaul was, in all probability, the ancient town of Çorbilo, which in those days was an important maritime centre at the mouth of the Loire in the Bay of Biscay. Balerium, we know from another source (Ptolemy), was Land's End.

One of the problems we have to decide is whether the above passage, with its strange interpolation of the appearance of " those islands that lie between Europe and Britain " so aptly descriptive of the Scillies, was merely a further reminder of the notable fact to those who dwelt in the Mediterranean where there are practically no tides, or whether Diodorus intended to explain that the tin was transported to France via a depôt on the Scilly Islands. Diodorus further mentions the three sources of tin in his time: " Tin is found in many parts of Iberia (Spain), not being discovered on the surface as some have babbled in their histories, but dug and smelted like silver and gold. For beyond the land of the Lusitanians (Portugal) are many mines of tin in the islands that lie off Iberia in the Ocean, which on this account are called the Cassiterides. And a great deal is brought from the British Island also to that part of Gaul that lies opposite; and across the midlands of the Celtic country it is brought on horseback to the people of Massilia (Marseilles) and to the town called Narbona. This is a colony of Romans which because of its fitness and its wealth, is the greatest place of exchange in those regions." Strabo tells us that " After the Romans had discovered a passage to these Islands (The Cassiterides), Publius Crassius, having sailed hither and seen them work their mines, which were not very deep, and that the people loved peace, and at their leisure, navigation also, instructed them to carry on this trade to better advantage than they had done before, though the Sea they had to cross was wider than betwixt it and Britain."

Canon Taylor, in his recent book on St. Michael's Mount, says: " there is only one point in his (Strabo's) narrative which is perplexing, viz., his concluding statement that the sea route is longer than that to Britain. He may mean that the distance by sea from the Mediterranean port to the Cassiterides is greater than that from the Cassiterides to Britain."

One authority explains the passage as meaning: "that the Cassiterides are farther removed from the coasts of Spain than the rest of the Southern coasts of Britain"; this explanation would only hold true if the Roman navigators sailed along the northern coast of France to within visible distance of Britain, and then crossed the Channel to continue a similar progress towards Cornwall. This seems unlikely at so late a date, when intercommunication was known to be frequent between the Belgae of Armorica Brittany) and Cornwall; moreover, Diodorus says that in B.C. 8 Balerium (Land's End) was four days' sail from the Continent. One of Caesar's excuses for invading Britain was that its natives sent assistance to West Gaul to resist him. The whole passage would be clear enough if the Scillies had been the depôt for Cornish tin. Publius Crassius, who was Cæsar's legate in Gaul, found that the tin was being transhipped by the Veneti, a maritime tribe inhabiting the mouth of the Loire and the coast of Armorica, who had something like a monopoly of the sea-carrying trade for some years before the Romans brought order into Gaul; Crassius would naturally desire to cut out the middlemen in Scilly and have the tin delivered direct to Gaul from St. Michael's Mount on its route to Marseilles. Might not the explanation be that Crassius instructed the Britons how to sail to Gaul rather than to the Scillies—though the sea they had to cross (to Gaul) "was wider than to Scilly"? We know that the Romans used the Scillies as a place of banishment for criminals or political offenders, and some accounts state that they were forced to work in the tin mines there!

The fact that St. Michael's Mount was used as a place of barter in the later period of the trade leads us to infer that the mainland was unsettled, and that the merchants needed the security afforded by small islands, which they could more easily defend, for the conduct of their, no doubt, protracted business of buying and selling. St. Michael's Mount, without its modern quay, was an exceptionally dangerous anchorage and there was no shelter whatever on any side of its rocky coastline, whereas St. Ives Bay and Falmouth Estuary would seem to have been ideal for their purpose.* The Mount, far from being a rival to the claim of the Scillies to the title of the original Cassiterides, demonstrates a feature of the times that must have been even more pronounced during the earlier and original traffic in tin.

It seems doubtful whether we shall ever know from whence originated the tin that was amongst the spoils of the Midianites, but a small quantity may have come via the overland route from India—undoubtedly tin was invaluable for making a cutting edge before iron came into use in the Mediterranean area about B.C. 1000—or it may have come, as we think, from the Scillies, and there is some evidence to show that tin is, and was, available on the islands. Geologically, the islands are very similar to West Cornwall, but the Scillies were definitely considerably larger, even within historical times, than they are now. It is not unreasonable to suppose that tin was, in fact, taken from the land that lay between the islands and is now covered by the sea. The early shallow mining pits would leave little evidence after so many ages, though there are indentations, notably on Tresco and St. Agnes, which some authorities claim to be evidence of excavations for tin; the adits of deeper mining operations are more uncertain, but there are several subterranean passages, such as Piper's Hole on Tresco, which may have been caused by human hand. A. Majendie, writing in the Royal Geological Society's Journal in 1818, mentioned that a small quantity of tin was raised at St. Mary's "about twenty years ago." The same

*The art of beaching ships of considerable tonnage, an art perfected by the Mediterranean sailors in the days of which we are writing, has been lost. It would seem, nevertheless, to have been highly improbable that ships could have been successfully beached on the rocky shores of the "Mount".

journal, in 1906, says that " many narrow oblong pits above Cromwell's Castle (Tresco) show where the tin was dug along the veins in the granite." The surveyors also found tin veins in the granite on the South side of St. Agnes.

There is an Indenture, dated as late as 1563, between Martin Dare, John Elliot and Roger Carew, for the joint working of tin mines in the Scilly Isles. Robert Heath, an officer of H.M. Forces stationed on Scilly, stated that " Several of these Islands afford tin, and some also, lead and copper. The tin is discoverable by the banks next the sea, where the marks of the ore in some places are visible upon the surface: this, I was assured by some very considerable Cornish miners, in the year 1744, who desired me to make representation thereof to the present proprietor, for obtaining his lordship's consent to their working of tin and other metals in Scilly." He adds that " a well opened in Hugh Town, opposite to the landing place, that had been filled up and out of use as long as the oldest in the island can remember, was cleared and, when the rubbish with which it was filled was removed, the miner discovered a rich vein of tin ore, which promised encouragement for working it as a tin work."

There is a further deduction to be made from the fact that the range of granite radiates from Devon to the Scillies and beyond, and that tin is most plentiful therewith on the extreme tip of land in Cornwall nearest to the Islands. Hencken clearly demonstrates from archaeological evidence that the most populous area in Cornwall, if not in Britain, from the Stone to the late Bronze ages, was the otherwise barren land contiguous to Land's End. We may reasonably infer, therefore, that the tin veins were nearer to the surface in that area than elsewhere on the mainland, and that they were more and more exposed as the range continues towards the Scillies. Here, then, tin would obtrude itself to the view of the natives long before it was recognised as a valuable article of trade and a search for other sources instigated.

There is no doubt that, in the course of time, the surface tin would be worked out and the Cornish tin would be exploited. There was at one time a notion that tin could never be exhausted, and Pliny says of tin that it is "fabulously (!) reported to grow in the Isles of the Atlantic Ocean and to be brought thence in wicker vessels, covered round with hides." Some writers have asserted that the early navigators wrongly assumed that Cornwall was an island and that, owing to the estuaries on the Southern coast of Britain, an appearance of a succession of islands is presented to a ship passing down the Channel, but such an assertion does not seem to be based on any other foundation, and we can safely assume that the traders were sufficiently inquisitive to visit them or obtain information from the natives, with whom they would very soon learn to converse on maritime matters.

It has been claimed that Hebrew, Phoenician and cognate languages had only one word to signify island, peninsulas, sea-coasts, and even remote countries, and that this fact misled the early historians. It is also argued that the Cassiterides included Britain, Ireland, and other islands, though Pliny says of the island called Britannia that it is "celebrated in the records of Greece and his own country." A further suggestion has been made that the Greeks named several of their metals after the country from which they came, and that the south of Ireland and the south-west of England were occupied by the race of Cessair (Kessair), a legendary heroine of the Castari tribe, who was said to be the granddaughter of Noah and the supposed earliest coloniser of Ireland. The Castari and Cassiterides are claimed to have some alliterative significance.

We have marshalled the main arguments that have been used by historians both for and against the connection of the Scilly Isles with the ancient tin trade and, though we appreciate that hardly any of the ancient writers came within a thousand miles of the parts of the world concerning which they were dealing, we think that the accounts they give disclose no glaring inconsistencies with our contention that for some hundreds of years the islands formed the tin trade depôt for the whole of the then known world.

THE ROMANS

THE area of Roman civilian settlement did not extend to Devon and Cornwall, and there are few traces of their time, but it is probable that they kept up a military establishment, since we have records of their making use of the Islands as a place of banishment for political offenders.

Although they had been very anxious to ascertain the whereabouts of the " Cassiterides " in former times when they occupied Britain, it is doubtful whether any tin was mined in the Islands or whether any vestige of the trade remained there, since the Roman arrival had been preceded, of course, by peace in Gaul, and the trade had then largely lost its maritime nature. Mr. Alexander Gibson, in his book on the Isles of Scilly, states that the Islands possess what no other place in the West Country can show, viz., a Roman altar, originally found on St. Mary's and now at Tresco. This is the only tangible evidence of Roman occupation, but there is said to be a paved causeway, now about six feet below the sea, between Crow Bar (St. Mary's) and Tresco; it is claimed to have been seen within living memory, and to consist of large flat stones; a possible continuation of the " Roman " road can be traced inland on St. Mary's.

The tradition arose, possibly, from the fact that St. Martin's and Tresco were one island and that the flats between were cultivated and that it was possible to walk along the ridge of Crow Bar to St. Mary's. The sea may have encroached from the East and a wall built to contain it. In the course of time this wall would have been abandoned and parts of its top appear to be flat to anyone looking downwards through water from a boat.

Some authorities have satisfied themselves that there is such a Causeway and that it is of Roman origin but no one has ever produced a theory to account for its existence. If however, it was a barrier against the encroaching sea, the conception of fighting against natural forces would seem to have been beyond the native inhabitants of the time, and Roman influence cannot be entirely discounted.

According to Camden, an iron spire, thought to have been erected by the Romans on a dangerous strag of ragged rocks, was thrown down by a storm in 1647. Some Roman coins have been unearthed on St. Mary's.

The Emperor Maximus transported " Instantius," a bishop of Spain, and " Tiberianus " to the " Insula Sylina quae ultra Britannias est " for heresy in the time of Priscillianus, anno 380. The Emperor Marcus banished a false prophet, during the time of the rebellion of Cassius, for " pretending to prophesy, and foretelling of things to come, as if he was inspired," and sent him to the " Silia Insula."

It has been claimed that Scilly ling, dried and salted, was regarded as a great delicacy at Roman banquets.

No doubt the " Pax Romana " was kept in Scilly, as elsewhere in Britain, during the long Roman occupation, and it may well be that Christianity and culture proceeded apace since, when the Northmen came later on, they found " priests and other learned men."

With the exception of Publius Crassius, who investigated the tin monopoly hitherto held by the Phoenicians, and the accounts of Strabo and other chroniclers of that time given in the chapter on the Tin Trades, there are no records, and it may be said that the Islands during this period " enjoyed profound tranquillity."

LYONESSE

Lyonesse has always been classed as a land of fable, largely because the tradition has inspired poets and writers to produce immortal stories connected with it which do not pretend to be other than fantasies of the imagination. When the poets' vision is discounted, nevertheless, there is some circumstantial evidence for the existence of the Land of Lyonesse which would incline the least imaginative of us to record a verdict of " not proven."

Such a verdict would be given, necessarily, to the story of the lost Atlantis, the " continent " that was swallowed by the Atlantic Ocean, and to the story of the lost Continent of Mu in the Pacific Ocean, and, also, to the legend that between Land's End and the Scillies there once existed a stretch of country containing no less than 140 villages and churches which, in one mighty cataclysm, was inundated for ever by the sea.

The sea-bed retains its secrets more effectively than does the land and, while scientists are enabled to discover cities and the evidences of past civilisations by a simple process of digging into the earth, the sea swamps every trace except that which is retained in the memory of man.

The main argument rests of course on the antiquity and the persistence of the story, which would represent the natural course of evidence necessarily handed down by word of mouth (as was the story of the Deluge in the Old Testament). The main feature would seem to be too important and circumstantial to have been the invention of one man, but which, nevertheless, is subject to embellishments as successive writers of prose and verse permit their imaginations to lead them on. Even to-day there are people who will tell you, in all seriousness, that, while crossing from Land's End, they have heard the church bells ringing below the sea!

And now let us consider the evidence.

Is it geologically possible? The answer must be that not only is it possible that the Islands were at one time attached to the mainland, but that it is almost certain that they were so attached, but whether this was in the time of "Homo Sapiens" we do not know.

Geographically, the Islands have the same granite formation as exists at Land's End and, in this connection, it is worth noting the fact that flints and chalk formations, exactly similar, are found on the Castle Downs of Tresco and at the Land's End, and are discovered there only at the precise points where the Islands and Mainland face each other, and where the disruption, granting it to have occurred, must have commenced.

The great granite mass which represents the foundation of the Scillies—which are, in effect, merely the protuberances on its summit—embraces an oval in which all the islands and rocks are included, from the Bishop to the Eastern Islands: in the centre is an outcrop of the firmer granite core of which the mass is composed, and surrounding it is a protective layer of blown sand and coarser grained granite which is in various stages of decomposition. Of the wearing property of granite, it has been said that the coarse grain will last for ever and the fine grain "a day longer."

Certain phenomena connected with the granite definitely associate the mass with that of the south-western portion of England, and are confined to those areas only. The occurrence of glacial deposit of chalk-flints and greensand-chert on the highest part of St. Martin's, are similar in constitution to the Eocene river-gravels of Devon and Dorset, and the Islands must have been the last relic of an old table-land over which the Eocene rivers radiating from Dartmoor, flowed outwards across what is now part of the Atlantic to the Continental shelf about 200 miles beyond the Scilly Islands.

In the Geological Survey, by George Barrow, which is published by H.M. Stationery Office, it is stated that the land in this part of the world has at various periods suffered subsidence, and also elevation; it is pointed out that the sand bar called Crow Bar that lies across Crow Sound, could only have been formed at a period when the sea was at least 25 feet below its present level. This deposit dates probably from Neolithic times, since human skulls and flint implements have been found in similar circumstances elsewhere, nearly 40 feet below the present sea-level. On the other hand, the islands must have been entirely submerged in Pliocene times!

The Survey summarises the different stages:—

"The following stages in the movements that have affected the Scilly Isles can be clearly established:—

(1) The formation of the Old Beach, at sea-level.

(2) The Old Beach was raised at least 40 feet.

(3 A comparatively recent subsidence has depressed the whole area of the South of Ireland, South Wales, Cornwall and the Scilly Isles at least 40 feet, for it has brought the Old Beach back again to sea-level; indeed, in the case of the Scilly Isles, almost to low-water mark."

Although we must take the word "recent" in this account in the sense that a geologist would use the word, it is interesting to note that the subsidence appears to be somewhat greater in Scilly than in the neighbouring land masses.

There appears to be some evidence of a further gradual subsidence, as witness the fine iron-cement—a natural product—around the margin of the Great Pool of Tresco which, although now below sea-level, is unbleached by the action of sea water and must therefore have been above high-water mark before the protecting sand bars were formed.

It is, however, comforting to read the final paragraph of the Survey:

"One point has been established in the clearest manner: the area above water in the Scilly Isles has not diminished in recent times, but has distinctly increased, and this increase is due to the constant washing up of the fine sand from the shallow sea-floor to the foreshore. From this position, in dry weather, it is blown further inland and so constantly continues the process of connecting one isolated island or islet with another, and sheltering the low-lying ground behind from the inroads of the sea.

The rock of the "Wolf," lying partway between Land's End and the Scillies, is composed of greenstone (slate), and seaweed brought out of the sea-bed between sometimes has greenstone attached to it; it is, however, improbable, as has been suggested from this circumstance, that the Island granite forms a distinct and separate range.

On the ten-fathom line, all present islands of the archipelago become hills on one large island about seven miles long and less than six miles wide, with a long, narrow peninsula projecting an additional three miles at an angle from one corner. The submergence may have been a gradual process through the ages.

The sea between the Mainland and the Seven Stones, and the Seven Stones and Scilly, is shallow—nowhere more than 50 fathoms. Great inundations of land on the coasts of Britain are known to have occurred within historic times, and one special invasion of the sea, about the close of the 11th Century, included the land that is now the Goodwin Sands and, almost certainly, the greater part of Mount's Bay from Cudden Point to Mousehole, and other parts of Cornwall and South Devon.

According to the old records this great inundation occurred in Autumn, leaves and hazel nuts being constantly found below the sands in Mount's Bay, and the stumps of trees observed under the water at low tides. St. Michael's Mount was once called " the Hore rock in the wood."*

Tradition may be wrong in details but rarely in outlines, and since this particular cataclysm is known to have affected Mount's Bay, how reasonable to assume that it altered the conformation of the Islands, not, however, at that period to the extent suggested in the Legend of Lyonesse (since we know that the Scillies were islands long before the 11th Century), but as the culmination of a series of lesser erosions or inundations. St. Michael's Mount was an appanage of St. Michael's Mount in Brittany, and modern writers are now largely agreed that the story of the " Wood " was borrowed from the parent abbey, though there may have been some local inundations.

Chronologically, there are several dates for which there is some evidence of a catastrophe, and it may well be that the Scilly Islands have suffered inundation or subsidence at several periods, a process that has continued, though mildly, at times within living memory.

Apart from the legend of Lyonesse and King Arthur, who is thought to have been King of West Britain in or about 540 A.D., Plutarch (120 A.D.) hints that the islands round Britain were generally unpeopled in his time, and this, in conjunction with Strabo's statement (circa B.C. 50) that " the Cassiterides are ten in number, close to one another, one of them is desert and unpeopled, the

*" Apparicio Sancti Michaelis in monte Tumba antea vocata le " Hore-rok in the Wodd "; et fuerunt tam boscus quam prata et terra arabilis inter dictum montem et insulae Sylle, et fuerunt 140 ecclesiae parochiales inter istum montem et Sylly submersae "; William of Worcester " viagio de Bristol ursque and montem St. Michaelis," dated 1478.

rest are inhabited," suggests that an inundation, which besides reducing the land may well have caused the islanders to emigrate to safer ground, may have occurred between those dates.

In 830 A.D., 1,000 persons are known to have been drowned on islands near Cork, Ireland, which is not far distant, and in 1014 A.D. (according to the "Saxon Chronicle") the land around St. Michael's Mount, Penzance, is reported to have been inundated and many people drowned.*

The "Saxon Chronicle," referring to the 11th November, 1099, states: "This year also on St. Martin's Mass-day the sea-tide ran up so very high and did so much harm as no one remembered that it ever before did; and it was the same day luna prima."

In Edward I's time (1272-1307) there is known to have occurred a great inundation or erosion of the sea at Old Winchelsea, near Rye, which may well have been part of a widespread disturbance.

It should be noted, however, that there is no record in the Annals of Tavistock Abbey (founded in 961), but to which St. Nicholas Abbey may not have been attached until about 1100 A.D., of any such occurrence.

In the Welsh Triads there is a story of a great inundation about 500 A.D. which totally destroyed nineteen of the largest fortified towns in Wales, which had been protected by a high embankment, the guardians of which fatally neglected their duty. A lament on this, attributed to Gwyddno Garanhir, is preserved in the "Myvyrian Archaeology":

*" Hoc item anno in vigilius Sancti Michaelis contigit magna ista Maris inundatio per latam hanc terram quot longius expatiata, quam antea unquam, demersit multa oppida et hominum inenarrabilem."

*" Stand forth, Seithenin,**
And behold the dwelling of heroes,
The plain of Gwyddno the ocean covers!
Accursed be the sea guard,
Who after carousel,
Let loose the destroying fountain of the raging deep!
A cry from the sea arises above the winds!
Even to heaven does it ascend,
After fierce excess comes the long cessation! . . . . . .
A cry from the sea arises above the winds!
A cry from the sea
Impels me from my place of rest this night!
After excess comes the far extending death! "

And what of the mysterious members of the group " Nurcho " or " Nutho," mentioned in a circumstantial document by Reginald de Dunstanville, Earl of Cornwall (1140-1175), and the doubtful identification of St. Lides; or the island called " Rentmen " that cannot be identified with any of the known Islands?

The islands were, without doubt, at one time considerably larger than they are today, and possessed a large population; how else can one account for the outlines of stone " hedges " and buildings now under the sea, and the great dumps of limpet and cockle shells?

The story that the great Saxon King, Athelstan, sailed personally with a great fleet to subdue them and, having done so, should have been so proud of his achievement that he is said to have founded the Collegiate Church of St. Buryan, near Land's End, to commemorate his victory, may have been due to a concentration of the Northmen who used the islands as a base, though there

*Seithenin—one of the three celebr ated drunkards of History.

is the possibility that his enemy consisted of natives, especially since his visit was the culmination of a long series of battles in Cornwall.

Leland, in 1538, mentions the circumference of Iniscaw (Tresco) as nine or ten miles* and adds that " wild boars roamed over it," but here there is some conflict of evidence since St. Mary's was called Ennor, meaning " Great Island," long before Leland's time.

That a tract of land called Lyonesse (or in Cornish, Lethowsow), existed as a partial or entire connection with the Mainland, is an article of faith with West Cornishmen and Scillonians and as a tradition will die hard; it is embellished with an account of a great town called the City of Lions at the Seven Stones, where the lightship is now stationed, and where the site is still spoken of as " The Town." They state that at the Seven Stones, small diamond-shaped panes, set in lead, and forming rude casements, have been found, and the tops of buildings observed under the sea! Heath states that " at Sennen Church-Town, near the extremity of Cornwall, there is the base of an old stone-column, belonging to a building, which was taken up by some fishermen, at the Place of the Seven Stones, about 18 inches height and 3 feet diameter at the circular base. Besides which, other pieces of building, and glass-windows, have been taken up at different times in the same place, with divers kinds of utensils . . . ." There is the tradition of the Trevillian (Trevelyan) family that bears a crest commemorating an ancestor who saved himself from his Lyonesse estates at the time of the inundation, by mounting his white horse which carried him to safety. Since crests have existed barely 700 years and the use of leaded lights is comparatively recent we must, if we are to believe them, fix the

*A mile was then the equivalent of 1½ miles to-day.

date of the minor inundations, if not of the major inundation, within historical times.

We know that erosion or inundation and perhaps a subsidence of the land, has taken place at various times, in some degree, both on the Islands and at Mount's Bay, and some of it within living memory. There is an interesting aerial photograph taken near Samson and showing the outline of walls and a house under what is now the sea. Tresco and Samson were undoubtedly joined together at one time.

Although we find historical records and reminiscences of many families having estates on the Scillies, such as the noble Norman House of Barentin, of Ranulph de Blankminster, John de Allet, and William de Poer, there are no mediæval remains, no ruins of great houses and not one sepulchral relic of any period between Druidical or Danish occupation and the great grandfathers of living men. This is one of the great unsolved mysteries in connection with the Islands; with the exception of some Norman arches in the ruins of Tresco Abbey, some traces at Old Town Church, and the ruins of the Church on St. Helen's, there is little indication of human activity between the late Bronze Age and the 16th Century.

The missing link between the Scillies and the Mainland originated with the story of King Arthur. The Ballads do not tell us when King Arthur and his Knights were defeated, but he himself is no legendary person, and according to some accounts he and his Queen Guinevere were buried at Glastonbury. It is said, when Henry II visited that monastery, that bones, some "of a marvellous bigness," were exhumed and an inscription found on a leaded cross: "Hic Jacet Sepultus Inclytus Rex Arturius in Insula Avallonia, cum Wennevereia uxore sua secunda."

Arthur, according to one, was the sovereign of the proper Silures (originally an Iberian tribe) and therefore denominated King of Gwent the " Venta Silurium " of the Romans, and British metropolis of the nation. He is said to have driven the Saxons into Scotland and gained great victories in Sussex and Wiltshire. To celebrate his achievements and the ensuing peace, he called a grand tournament —the tilting ground afterwards became known as the Round Table—and established a military order " to call forth all the worth of the nation and collect it round the Pendragon of the Lord of the British Confederacy." Civil war, however, broke out and dashed his hopes to the ground. " Thus died King Arthur 542 A.D., and with him ended the happiness of Britain."

Malory refers to Surluse or Surluce, as part of the kingdom of Lyonesse, of which Sir Galahalt " the haut prince of Surluce " was ruler under King Arthur, and to whom he had to apply for sanction before he could so much as stage a tournament; elsewhere Sir Galahalt is mentioned as " of the Long Isles " the inhabitants of which were Silures, who had Iberian blood in their veins, were dark and swarthy with curled hair and were known to be hardy fighters.

No less an authority than Baring Gould says that the real Lyonesse was in Brittany in the realm of Leon, so called because founded by colonists from Caerleon, the City of Legions, in South Wales, who fled from the swords of the Saxons.

Detractors of this story of a lost land will say that such a great catastrophe, if it occurred within historical times, would have been recorded from many sources, especially since the effects of such a convulsion of nature could hardly have been confined to one locality, and that it gained credence from de Malory's romantic story of the Knights of the Round Table and the story of King Arthur, later used by Tennyson, who visited the Isles to compose his immortal poems. The story has inspired many poets and writers in Brittany and England, including Milton, Spencer, Dryden, Scott, Swinburne and William Morris.

All of us who possess a streak of romanticism will cling to the belief, regardless of probability, in company with Spencer, that " fertile Lyonesse " really did exist once upon a time, " on the confines of faery land."

THE STORY OF KING ARTHUR

"So all day long the noise of battle roll'd
Among the mountains by the winter sea;
Until King Arthur's Table, man by man,
Had fall'n in Lyonesse about their Lord,
King Arthur . . . ." TENNYSON.
("Morte d'Arthur")

No book on the Scillies would be complete without a reference to that undying romance of the days of chivalry, related by Sir Thomas Maleor, when Britain belonged to the British, and King Arthur reigned at his Castle at Tintagel over all the land from Devon, Cornwall, Lyonesse and finally Cassiteris (afterwards called Scilly), which provided the final scene of this noble tragedy.

Geoffrey of Monmouth (Bishop of St. Asaph) introduced to the world the story of King Arthur; Arthur—"Emperor and Conductor of the Toil"—is one of the legendary heroes of the Britons (as was "Hercules" to the Tyrians) and he was the leader of the Celts who fought the Saxon invaders in Britain and Brittany. "He defended his people against the Saxon invader, and their faith against the idolatry of Odin." He is said to have fought twelve great battles ending with that of Camlon (which may have been Camelon, on the Carron in Stirlingshire, or on the Camel in Cornwall), and to have been buried in Avalon (which the Bretons claim to be in Brittany), or Glastonbury—if he was buried at all! J. C. Walters has said that "Arthur's graves are so many that it would be easy to reduce the whole thing to an absurdity by saying, that if there were a doubt that King Arthur ever lived, his numerous "graves" conclusively prove that he died many times, despite the tradition, too, that he did not die at all!"

In a poem of Layamon, Arthur is made to say, after bearing fifteen wounds: "But I will press to Avalon, to the fairest of all maidens, to Argente the Queen, an elf most beautiful, and she shall make my wounds all whole with draughts of healing. And afterwards I will come again to my Kingdom." Bretons believe that "he liveth yet and wonneth in Avalon, with the fairest of Queens of Faery."

"The name of King Arthur has been perpetuated in more place-names and local association (says the learned Dr. Dickinson) than any other person, save only the devil!" In the British Isles alone, more than 600 localities cherish traditions of King Arthur, and Lord Bacon remarks that "in the acts of King Arthur there is enough to make him famous, besides that which is fabulous."

He is also associated with the search for the Holy Grail which, in Celtic legend, was a vessel as rich in food, and as inexhaustible, as the purse of Fortunatus in gold, but conceived by the writers of romance to be a mystic dish or cup used by our Lord before His Passion, and to be still existent.

King Arthur, living in the Dark Ages, had no chronicler, probably no one in all his realm who could read or write, save perhaps a few semi-literate priests; no contemporary manuscript has come down to us to record his saga, and no ballads or verse that his story should be preserved intact, without the exaggerations that are apparently inseparable from stories that have no set form, as when they are recorded in script. According to one account he "was made Kinge of all Brittaine when hee was butt of XV years of age, butt hee was faire and boulde, and doughtye of bodie, and to meke folk hee was good and curteous, and lardg of spending, and made hyme wonderouslie well beloved among all men were it was neede."

The final battle of his reign was against his kinsman Mordred, said to be King of the Picts and Scots: "Never (says one chronicler) was there seen a more dolefuller battle in no Christian land: for there was but rushing and riding, foining and striking, and many a grim word was there spoken either to other and many a deadly stroke. But always King Arthur rode throughout the battle of Sir Mordred many times, and did there right nobly as a noble king should do; and at all times he never fainted."

The following legend is taken from that of the Rev. H. Whitfield, M.A., published in 1852 in "Scilly and its legends":

"It will be remembered that, after the valiant wars that King Arthur and his Knights of the Round Table had waged on behalf of the Confederacy, he returned to Tintagel and, together with his paladins, held high court, but at that time the spirit of the assembled knights, alas much diminished in numbers, and the spirit at the court, was not what it once had been. There were ominous rumours that his kinsman, Prince Mordred, had banded together all those who resented King Arthur's high-handed actions, all the malcontents and those whose evil designs had been frustrated, and that this army was preparing to march on him at his very castle of Tintagel itself.

"This was civil war, some of the flower of his own chivalry, knights who had been trained by King Arthur himself and who had fought with him in many a mighty battle, and led by a prince of his own blood, and, sternly and slowly, as though dreading that which they were about to do, the mighty host of his enemies advanced towards Cornwall.

" And, as the array drew near, King Arthur with his veterans, Sir Lancelot and Sir Tristram, Sir Banyan and Sir Bor, Sir Ector and Sir Cote mal taillé, Sir Caradoc and Sir Percival and their followers, marched out to meet them.

" Alas, rebellion has no shame, it grows more bitter for its very baseness, and fiercer for the badness of its cause and, on the evening of that day, King Arthur lay dead on the plain and the remnants of the Knights of the Round Table, hopelessly out-numbered, fled, through inhospitable Cornwall, to that fair wide tract of country called, in the Cornish tongue " Lethowsow " (Lyonesse).

" These jaded knights, with a few kindred followers, were all that was left of the flower of Britain's chivalry, and all that they carried with them was the knowledge of defeat and the banner, torn and bloody, that had covered the breast of their beloved king and, as they went, fleeing for their lives, the host of Mordred thundered on their rear.

" By the side of the road, not far from the spot where in after days the piety of Athelstan founded the college and church of St. Buryan, there dwelt a holy hermit. In his poor cell one of the knights, whose wounds were mortal, laid down and departed from life. As the hermit knelt and prayed by his body, Mordred rode up. His face was pale as death, and was rendered still more ghastly by a blue livid wound, that traversed his whole forehead, and was lost amid his hair, matted and soaked with blood. He dismounted and entered the hut. The hermit and the dead man were its only tenants save him. He looked upon the face of the corpse. It was the face of an early comrade of his own. The same blood ran in the veins of their mothers. He turned gloomily away and signed the sign of the cross, involuntarily, upon his breast. The hermit sighed when he beheld the action. " Alas," said he to Mordred, " thou hast in one day done more evil than all thy ancestry have ever in their whole lives done of good. The crown of Arthur is upon thy brow, but the brand of Cain is there also. Go on, thou traitor to God and man." And Mordred smote him angrily with his gauntlet. " Go on," added the recluse, " thy course is well nigh done. The shadow of a mighty one is brooding over thee. Go on, and die." And Mordred mounted his horse and urged it furiously forward. But the animal refused to obey the spur. The power of that dread spirit was before him. It had far more terrors for the charger than bit or steel. The avenging spectre would not give place to man's worth. After a long and ineffectual struggle the might of the unearthly prevailed. The ghastly chase was resumed, with the same dogged sullenness as before.

" And now Mordred reached a lofty slope, from which, more clearly than he had hitherto been able to do, he could see his retiring enemies. They were already at a very considerable distance, upon that winding road which then led over the fertile tract of country called in Cornish " Lethowsow," or, in after-days, " Lyonesse." They were so far in advance that he could only follow their course by catching at intervals the gleaming of their arms. Around him was that fair land, now so long lost and forgotten, from the bosom of which men for ages had dug mineral wealth, upon which were seen no fewer than one hundred and forty stately churches, and whose beauty and fruitfulness have been the theme of many a romantic lay. Broken sunlight floated over its soft glades. It never looked so grandly glorious as on that hour of its fate. As Mordred pressed on, full of one thought alone, already in imagination hemming into slaughter or driving into the waves his enemies, his attendants and followers began to be sensible of a change in the atmosphere, of a something oppressive and horrible, though he himself perceived it not.

"Huge battlemented clouds, tinged with lurid red, hung over the horizon. The air became sultry and choking. A tremulous and wavy motion shook the ground at intervals. A low sound, like distant thunder, moaned around. The soldiers of his train drew closer together, awe-struck and terrified. But Mordred heard only the evil voice of his own passions. The war of the elements gave unmistakable signs of its awaking. But Mordred perceived it not.

"At last, amid a silence that might be felt, so dreadful was it, and so dull—that fearful shade, which had hitherto gone before him, and restrained his madness, suddenly itself stopped. It assumed a definite shape. It was the form of Merlin, the Enchanter. But it was even more terrible than Merlin, for it united the earthly glare of the spectre with the grandeur of the inspired man.

"Right in Mordred's path, face to face, did the avenger stand. They remained for a few seconds, motionless, frowning upon each other. Neither spoke, save with the eye. After those few seconds, the great wizard raised his arm. Then there ensued a confused muttering, a sound as though the foundations of the great deep were broken up. Soon the voice of the subterranean thunder increased, and the firm soil beneath their feet began to welk and wave, and fissures appeared upon the surface, and the rock swelled like the throes of a labouring sea.

"With a wild cry of agony, the band of pursuers became in turn the pursued. They wheeled and rushed away in headlong flight. But it was in vain. The earth, rent in a thousand fragments, in the grasp of that earthquake, upheaved its surface convulsively, gave one brief and conscious pause, and then, at once sank down for ever beneath the level of the deep. In a moment a continent was submerged, with all its works of art, and piety, with all its living tribes, with all its passions, and hopes, and fears.

"The soldiers of Mordred were whirled away in the stream created by that sudden gulf, which even now flows so violently over its prey below. Last of all, Mordred remained, as it were, fascinated and paralyzed, gazing at the phantom with a look in which horror struggled with hate, and which was stamped with scorn and defiance to the end.

"That morning had dawned upon as bright a scene as ever met the eye. At evening there was nought—from what was then first termed the Land's End to St. Martin's head—but a howling and boiling wilderness of waves, bearing here and there upon its bosom a fragment from the perished world beneath or a corpse tossed upon the billows over which sea-birds wheeled and screamed.

"The remnant that was preserved reached in safety Cassiteris, called afterwards Silura, and now Scilly. There the wicked cease to trouble, and the weary were at rest.

"In their island home, upon which still the sea encroaches daily, they dwelt securely. From St. Martin's height, on their arrival, they saw the catastrophe that overwhelmed their enemies, and, dismounting, knelt upon the turf and thanked God for their deliverance. They never more sought the Britain of their hope and fame. It would have been a changed and melancholy home for them. Arthur was in his tomb at Glastonbury; Guenevere was dead. The Round Table was broken and its best knights perished or dispersed. Their work was done.

"In the Isles of Scilly, miraculously severed from the mainland, and as it were set apart for their sakes, they lived, and there they died. In after days their children raised a stately religious house, at Tresco, over their bones. But their memory gradually faded away and was forgotten. Sometimes on a clear day there may be seen the remains of walls or buildings under the sea. Sometimes fishermen bring up relics of other times and men wonder at them and speculate upon their cause and use. Strangers make pilgrimages to Scilly, and marvel whether it ever exceeded its present limits. But the accounts of its isolation is remembered only as a confused dream; it is a mystery, an old-world tale; a fragment of which, like a portion of a wreck, floats about, here and there, in the visions of the past.

"Such is the legend of the Lyonesse."

"*Then rose the King and moved his host by night,*
And ever push'd Sir Mordred, league by league,
Back to the sunset bound of Lyonesse—
A land of old upheaven from the abyss
By fire, to sink into the abyss again;
Where fragments of forgotten peoples dwelt,
And the long mountains ended in a coast
Of ever-shifting sand, and far away
The phantom circle of a moaning sea."

—TENNYSON.
("*The Passing of Arthur.*")

THE VIKINGS AND SAXONS

When the Romans—who had policed the Britains so effectually that they had lost the arts of war and the spirit to defend themselves—were retired to the Continent to defend the heart of the Empire from the Goths, the Scillies, together with the rest of Britain, were left defenceless. For 400 long years we hear nothing of the Scillies except that they formed a base for the marauding Northmen, who undoubtedly were joined by the Celtic-speaking Welshmen of Cornwall, and probably by the Iberian settlers of the Scillies and Penzance. The "English" invaded Cornwall in 814, but it is not known whether they reached the Islands.

In 928, the Saxon King Athelstan, after making his orisons at St. Buryan, embarked with his fleet from Whitsand, near Plymouth, and succeeded in conquering the Islands; he is said to have left a garrison and, on his return, to have founded the Collegiate Church of St. Buryan in Cornwall as a thank-offering. The garrison must have been small, or perhaps it did not remain, because we hear nothing further of them. By this time, possibly as a result of the arrival of Benedictine or other monks from Ireland, the islands had adopted Christianity.

One account says that at the period there was a famous Abbot, the head of a great cloister, on Tresco, together with a "goodly company of monks." It is probable that the Abbey of St. Nicholas, portions of which are extant on Tresco, was founded in the tenth century. St. Nicholas, the saint chosen as patron, was a singularly appropriate choice since he was reported to preserve vessels in a miraculous manner when his aid had been fervently invoked; perhaps the "right of wreck" was given to the Monastery for the purpose of attaching an increased degree of merit to the prayers in favour of ships in danger.

St. Nicholas had also delegated to him from Heaven the peculiar care of infants, as a reward for his early piety, which induced him, in the first month, to abstain from taking the nourishment afforded by his mother's breast, on Wednesdays and Fridays and on all occasional fasts appointed by the Church. He was Archbishop of Myra, a city of Lycia in Lesser Asia, where he died in 342 A.D., his relics are now in the town of Bari, in Italy, where they continue to perform the most miraculous cures, more especially in the case of infants.

Into this "goodly company of Monks," this refuge of holy men of Ireland, Cornwall and the West, perhaps garrisoned by Saxons, and no doubt reinforced by doughty anchorites, who were, in those days, known to be as handy with the sword as with their beads, there descended 97 ships, a marauding army of Northmen, who, for four long years had been harrying, burning and slaughtering along the west coast of Scotland, England, Wales and the north coast of France.

The following is the account of Snorri Sturluson, written circa 1222, of events that are estimated to have taken place in the year 980, and translated by William Morris and Eirikr Magnusson. The story is from what is now called the "Heimskringla" (The Round World), and is one of the best-known Sagas of the old Norse kings:

> "Olaf Tryggvason was three winters in Wendland; and then Geira, his wife, fell sick, and that sickness brought her to her bane. Such great scathe did Olaf deem this that he had no love for Wendland ever after. So he betook him to his war-ships, and fared yet again a-warring; and first he harried in Friesland, and then about Saxland, and so right away to Flanders. Then

sailed Olaf Tryggvason to England, and harried wide about the land; he sailed north all up to Northumberland, and harried there, and thence north-away yet to Scotland, and harried wide about. Thence sailed he to the South-isles, and had certain battles there; and then south to Man, and fought there, and harried also wide about the parts of Ireland. Then made he for Bretland, and that land also he wasted wide about, and also the land which is called of the Kymry; and again thence sailed he west to Valland, and harried there, and then sailed back east again, being minded for England, and so came to the isles called Scillies in the Western parts of the English Main.

"Olaf Tryggvason was four winters about this warfare, from the time he fared from Wendland till when he came to Scilly.

"Now when Olaf Tryggvason lay at Scilly he heard tell that in the isle there was a certain soothsayer who told of things not yet come to pass; and many men deemed that things fell out as he foretold. So Olaf fell a-longing to try the spaeing of this man, and he sent to the wise man him who was fairest and biggest of his men, arrayed in the most glorious wise, bidding him say that he was the king; for hereof was Olaf by then become famed in all lands, that he was fairer and nobler than all other men. But since he fared from Garth-realm, he had used no more of his name than to call him Oli, and a Garth-realmer. Now when the messenger came to the sooth-sayer and said he was the king, then got he this answer: "King art thou not; but my counsel to thee is, that thou be true to thy king."

"Nor said he more to the man, who fared back and told Olaf thereof; whereby he longed the more to meet this man, after hearing of such answer given; and all doubt fell from him that the man was verily a soothsayer. So Olaf went to him, and had speech with him, asking him what he would say as to how he should speed coming by his kingdom, or any other good-hap.

"Then answered that lone-abider with holy spaedom: 'A glorious king shalt thou be, and do glorious deeds; many men shalt thou bring to troth and christening, helping thereby both thyself and many others; but to the end that thou doubt not of this mine answer, take this for a token: Hard by thy ship shalt thou fall into a snare of an host of men, and battle will spring thence, and thou wilt both lose certain of thy company, and thyself be hurt; and of this wound shalt thou look to die, and be borne to ship on shield; yet shalt thou be whole of thy hurt within seven nights, and speedily be christened thereafter.'

"So Olaf went down to his ship, and met unpeaceful men on the way, who would slay him and his folk; and it fared with their dealings as that lone-abiding man had foretold him, that Olaf was borne wounded on a shield out to his ship, and was whole again within seven night's space.

"Then deemed Olaf surely that the man had told him a true matter, and that he would be a soothfast soothsayer, whencesoever he had his spaedom. So he went a second time to see this soothsayer, and talked much with him, and asked him closely whence he had the wisdom to foretell things to come. The lone-dweller told him that the very God of christened men let him know all things that he would, and therewithal he told Olaf many great works of Almighty God; from all which words Olaf yeasaid the taking on him of christening; and so was he christened with all his fellows.

" He abode there long and learned the right troth, and had away with him thence 'priests and other learned men.'

" In the autumn-tide sailed Olaf from the Scillies to England. He lay in a certain haven there, and fared peacefully, for England was christened, as he was now christened."

King Olaf carried his new creed to Norway, Sweden, Denmark and Iceland and enforced it at the point of the sword!

" *King Olaf from the doorway spoke:*
' Choose ye between two things my folk,
To be baptised or given up to slaughter! "

—LONGFELLOW.

The mention of "priests and other learned men" is particularly interesting and opens up a field of conjecture; unfortunately, no other supporting evidence can be produced to confirm the implications.

This Saga is almost the last we hear of the Vikings; the monks of Scilly may well have been proud of their success in contributing to the history of Christianity, but, in order that they should not become too presumptuous, the great god Odin gave them one parting shot—we read that in A.D. 1155 one Svein Ashlifarson, " King of Orkney and Caithness," raided St. Mary's and " took much plunder."

FROM ATHELSTAN TO QUEEN ELIZABETH

CHRISTIANITY, which may have been imported at a very early date, probably from Greece, even before the Roman occupation—since communication with the Mediterranean must have been continuous—was, we know from various sources, well established in the eleventh century.

By the time of Edward the Confessor (1042-1066) there was a Priory at Tresco dedicated to St. Nicholas, and communicating by a road over dry land with a church at St. Helen's (this church has been dated by antiquarians as probably of sixth century foundation). We find records of cells and chapels bearing the names of St. Theona, St. Ruman and St. Mary. There are traces of similar institutions in other parts, as at Holy Vale—where there is said to have existed a convent—at Church Edge, at Monk's Port and Carn-Friars.

All these unrelated spiritual efforts eventually came under the control of Tavistock Abbey in the time of Henry I; and the possessions of the monks, and presumably the tithes (omnes Ecclesias de Sullye) were absorbed into the cell established at Tresco.* The exclusive ownership of St. Elid's (St. Helen's), St. Sampson (Samson), St. Teon (Teän), Reutmen (possibly Tresco), and Nurcho, or Nullo (unidentified) were included in the grant, together with all wrecks, except whole ships or whales (in these grants, gold, whale, scarlet cloth, fir and masts were always reserved to the King). In another grant all the tithes of Scilly (and particularly of rabbits) are given to the monks by Richard de Wick "for his soul and the souls of his parents, and of Reginald, Earl of Cornwall, his lord."

*It has been stated that St. Patrick enjoined a levy of a tithe of the men as well as a tithe of the land for the support of the church, but one-third of a monk's day was required to be spent in manual labour.

Reginald de Dunstanville, a natural son of Henry I, was created Earl of Cornwall in 1140 and confirmed the original grant to Tavistock Abbey, from which circumstance it follows that the Islands were then held as part of the Earldom.

From the time of its establishment to the Dissolution (1539), St. Nicholas' Abbey was controlled at different times by thirty-eight Abbots. We know little of their affairs but at one time they are said to have levied tolls on all who landed on the Islands, and they were constantly at loggerheads with the military and civil authorities. The traces of the Abbey which are still in existence would appear to indicate that the Abbey was of some considerable size, but the record of its destruction is missing and we can but surmise from the evidence of some charred timber that has been unearthed, that it was at some period destroyed by fire.

From a Return of Edward I Commissioners (1275) for the Hundred of Penwith it is stated that: " They (the Jury) say that John Dulet (of Alet in Kenwyn) and the Prior of St. Nicholas (Tresco), Lords of Scilly, take wreck of the sea in those Islands, but they know not by what warrant, the ancestors of the aforesaid John and the Prior having done so from the time whereof memory is not."

In the 30th year of Edward I we find the Abbot of Tavistock claiming " all Shipwrecks happening in all the Islands, which he and his predecessors had enjoyed without interruption from time immemorial."

The Monks must have been sorely harassed by marauders, since the Civil Authority could not, or would not, give the Islands the necessary protection.

Some interesting sidelights are however available, which give us a fairly good idea of the conditions. We find the monks complaining at the rigours of their existence on the Islands, and petitioning to be redrafted to the Parent Abbey; possibly a tour of duty on Scilly was used occasionally as a disciplinary measure or a penance. In the time of Edward III this Priory, or Cell, of Tavistock Abbey must have been of very little importance, since, in the 19th year of his reign, it appears that two monks only were resident; for some reason which it is difficult to appreciate, only secular priests were to be stationed in Scilly during the continuance of the war with France.

The following document, translated from the Norman-French, gives an interesting side-light on the Scillies as a resort and refuge of fugitive serfs in the time of Edward III. "Edward the (Black) Prince, etc. to Walter Hull, Constable of the Castle and Keeper of the Isles of Scilly:—At the suggestion of our well-beloved Ralph Vyvyan, one of our tenants in Cornwall, we command you that whereas Robert Martyn, Roger Tregarn, Robert Carngonel, and others his born serfs have run away out of his seignory in Cornwall as far as the said Isles, and now remain there. We command that if it be so, you permit that he take them again, and cause them to return to his seignory as Law and Right require, and do not make any disturbance or maintenance by them against him in this matter to his disinheritance. Done under our Privy Seal at London, the 4th February, 27 Edward III."

In a document (the Register of Bishop Grandison, dated 21st September, 1351), mention is made of the impoverishment occasioned to the said Abbey (Tavistock) from the enormous devastations recently committed by Pirates in Insula de Sully—"ex qua non modica pars subsidii Monasterii de Tavistock provenire consuerit."

We have seen that the secular authority was vested in the Earls of Cornwall in the time of Henry I, but it is not always easy to draw a distinction between ecclesiastic and secular affairs. One of the earliest known records is that of Pope Celestin III in 1193 confirming to the Abbey of

Tavistock its privileges and properties, and amongst them, within the Isles of Scilly, the Isle of St. Nicholas (Tresco), St. Sampson, St. Elidius, St. Theona the Virgin, and an island called Nutho (Nurcho) with their belongings, and all churches and oratories in all the isles, with tithes and offerings, besides two bits of wooded land in Aganus (Hagness, now St. Agnes) and three in Ennor (now St. Mary's). The Abbot is to be protected in his possessions against all assailants, his Bishop in particular (!) and for this exempton the Abbey has to pay yearly to the Roman Pontiff three golden pieces.

Scilly was a Feudal Lordship appurtenant and owing allegiance to the Castle of Launceston, and the Tenant owed suit and paid yearly a rent called "waiternfee" (or "Watching Fee") at Michaelmas at the Gate of the Castle.

The date of the building of Ennor Castle is uncertain, but it probably commenced in the time of Henry III (1126-1172) and may have been in existence earlier; it is mentioned specifically in a document dated 1244. This Castle, of which few vestiges remain, has been identified as Old Town Castle and was situated in a commanding position close to what was then the landing place and the main town. (This town was called Heyugcastle and gives a clue to the derivation of the word "Hugh.") Ennor or Ynnor was the secular name for St. Mary's and is probably a corruption of Ennis Moor, the great island, a name that ceased to be used after the fourteenth century.

In A.D. 1248, Dreux de Barrantine was sent to Scilly by Henry III to act as Governor and to administer justice; he receiving lands to the value of £10 in payment. The noble Norman Barrantines were a maritime family, keeping as long as they could to the sea coast; they held the Channel Islands under the Crown. The garrison of Ennor Castle would appear to have consisted of armed men supplied by tenants as a condition of holding land. The following are quoted by E. J. Barth Ennor in the Scillonian Magazine:—

"At Lanstaveton (Launceston) 17th April, 1244, before Justices itinerant and other liegemen of our lord the King then there present. Between Lawrence S. of Richard, claimant, and John de Lideford opponent; as to 1 ploughland in Agnas (St. Agnes, Scilly). Plea of warranty of charter as called on. John acknowledged the 1 ploughland to be the right of Lawrence, as that which Lawrence had by John's gift. To have and to hold to Lawrence and his heirs, of John and his heirs, for ever. Rendering therefore yearly 1 pair of white gloves or 1d. at Easter, and finding 2 servants with arms for ward of Ynnor Castle from the invention of the Holy Cross (3rd May) to the feast of St. Peter ad Vincula (1st August) for all service, custom, suit of court and exaction."

For this Lawrence gave to John 100 marks of silver.

"At Westminster, 3rd February, 1259, between Alan Bloyhon, plaintiff, and Ranulph de Albo Monasterio and Isabella his wife, tenants, by Reginald Bage in Isabella's place; as to 1 ploughland in Ineor (Ennor, *i.e.*, St. Mary's, Scilly)."

Alan acknowledged the said land to be the right of Isabella and remitted and quit claimed the same for himself and his heirs, to Ranulph and Isabella and the heirs of Isabella for ever.

For this Ranulph and Isabella give Alan 1 sore sparrow hawk!

Edward I granted the Castle of Ennor in Scilly to Ranulph de Blankminster—sometimes referred to as R-de Blanco Ministerio or de Albo Monasterio (or Whitchurch)—in return for finding twelve armed men, at all times to keep the peace, and paying yearly at Michaelmas three hundred puffins, or six and eightpence! This rent of

6s. 8d. seems to have been paid yearly up to the time of Edward VI (1547), but always in the form of money.

The Patent Rolls of Edward I describe the Castle as follows: " Island of Syley . . . The Castle of Ewer there is held of the Lords the King by the Service of finding and supporting 12 men-at-arms in the same Castle at all times." In the year 8 Edward II (1314-1315) Ranulph Blancminster had Licence to crenellate " mansum suum de Ivor." The Caption of Seizin preserved in the Duchy Office states that when the Black Prince took possession of his Duchy, the Lord of the " Manor of Sully " was at that time Ranulf of Blancminster who died Midsummer, 1348, leaving as his heir his grandson Gandewen, a minor of about nine years of age. The Duchy held the Manor during the Minority, and after an interval the Black Prince granted its custody and the wardship of the heir to William of Morier, or Morrers.

In the Minister's Accounts for the year 1348-9, the collection of rents by the Duchy is recorded. The rents collected were from Bond and Free Tenants, Perquisites of Court, Heriots and Rent for ships calling at the Islands, and a note is appended that the collection was " no more, because the great part of the Fishermen have died this year by the Pestilence."

A further account of the same Roll states that: " The Yearly Rents of 100s. for the Wine Tavern (Taberna vini, possibly a toll booth or Custom House) and of 40s. for the Windmill were not forthcoming because both tenements had been destroyed by the Foreigners."

In 1342, 600 Welshmen were sent to Brittany on the King's Service, and no doubt fought later at Crécy. We learn about them, not from a Writ of Array, but from a petition of the Lord of the Isles of Scilly (Patent Rolls) setting forth that " whereas these Welshmen were drawn by the sea on to that Island staying there for 20 days and carrying away £500 worth of crops, the Tenants are not able to till their lands and pay their dues."

From the Inquisition Post Mortem of the 22nd year of Edward III, it appears that " Ranulf of Blancminster held in his demesne as of fee of the Lord Edward Prince of Wales, Duke of Cornwall and Earl of Chester, as of the Honour of His Castle of Launceston, the Castle of Scilly with the Islands belonging to the said Castle by Knight Service at a yearly rent of 300 poffons or half a mark. The which Castle with the islands aforesaid are worth yearly in all issues according to the true value £18 19s. 4½d. ! "

Puffins would appear to have been valued for their feathers as much as their doubtful edible qualities; the normal value of puffins seemed to have increased, for, instad of 6s. 8d. (or 300 puffins), in the year 1440 it was 6s. 8d. (or 50 puffins). This Blankminster seems to have been a high-handed individual who, according to William le Poer, Coroner of St. Mary's, instead of keeping the peace, entertained rogues, thieves and felons and with their help committed many abuses. For this complaint Edward I appointed a commission, but nothing came of it, and William le Poer was thrown into prison by Blankminster at Le Val (probably Holy Vale) and made to pay one hundred marks. Justice was rough in those days, for instance:—

" John de Allet and Isabella, his wife, hold the Isle of Scilly and hold there all kinds of pleas of the crown throughout their jurisdiction and make indictments of felonies. When any one is attainted of any felony, he ought to be taken to a certain rock (said to be that on which " The Bishop " now stands), in the sea, with two barley loaves and one pitcher of water upon the same rock, they leave the same felon until, by the flowing of the sea, he is swallowed up."

We have another reference to the administration of the Blankminsters, in this case probably that of his son and successor, John de Albo Monasterio, Knight, and M.P. for the County of Cornwall in the year 47 of Edward III (1363-1364). In 1367 the priory of St. Nicholas having complained that for want of proper protection, it was wasted and improverished by the frequent arrival of the sea-ships of all nations, King Edward III, holding it in great esteem as a royal foundation, commands all dukes, earls, admirals, soldiers, masters of ships, and mariners, and especially " the constable of his castle in the isle of Ennor, to extend to the prior, monks, chaplains and their servants, all possible protection, so that they may be able to bear their proper burdens and offer prayers and devotions continuously for the King, his progenitors, and his heirs, as they had been wont to do."

The Blankminsters were succeeded by the Coleshills, and St. Agnes was held by the Hamely family for a considerable length of time, apparently as inferior grantees. On March 25th, 1351, Ralph Hamely granted to his brother Laurence, the Island of Agnes in Scilly, with the rents and services of the same, consisting of dried fish and wrecks of the said Island, paying yearly for seven years to come, one grain of wheat and after that time one hundred shillings Sterling.

William of Worcester in his itinerary of 1478 mentions the islands, and Richard III ordered an inquisition of them to be taken in 1484 when it appears that they were worth in time of peace, forty shillings, but in time of war—nothing!

The next important record is taken from the notes of John Leland, the antiquarian who visited Scilly shortly after the accession of Edward VI, in 1538, but who was prevented owing to loss of reason, from arranging them. Some of his notes are of great interest:—

" St. Mary Isle is a five miles or more in cumpace, in it is a poor town, and a meately strong pile (Ennor Castle); but the roves of the buildings in it be sore defacid and woren.

" Iniscaw longid to Tavestoke, and ther was a poor cell of monks of Tavestoke. Sum caulle this Trescaw; it is the biggest of the islettes, in cumpace 6 miles or more, it is inculta cum cuniculis et avibus vocatis pophyns.

" S. Agnes Isle so caullid of a chapel theryn.

" The Isle of S. Agnes was desolated by this chaunce in recenti hominum memoria. The hole numbre of V. housoldes that were yn this isle cam to a mariage or a fest in S. Mary Isle, and going homewarde were al drownid.

" Saynet Lides Isle wher yn tymes past at her sepulchre was gret superstition.

" Few men be glad to inhabite these islettes, for al the plenty, for robbers by sea that take their catail by force. The robbers be Frenchmen and Spaniardes.

" One Danvers a gentilman of Wilshir whos chief house at Daundsey, and Whitington, a gentilman of Glocestreshire be owners of Scylley; but they have scant 40 marks (£26 13s. 4d.) by yere of rentes and commodities of it.

" In the biggest isle (cawled St. Nicholas Isle) of the Scylleys ys a lytle pyle or fortres, and a paroch chyrche that a monke of Tavestoke yn peace doth serve as a membre of Tavestoke Abbay. Ther be yn that paroch about LX howseholdes. The ground of this isle berith exceeding corn; insomuch that if a man do but cast corn wher hogges have rotid it wyl cum up.

" Ther is a nother cawled Inisschawe, that ys to say the Isle of Elder, by cause yt berith stynkkyng elders. Ther be wild bores or swyne.

" Ther is one isle of the Scylleys cawled Rat Isle, yn which be so many rattes that yf horse, or any other lyving beast be brought thyther, they devore him. Ther is a nother cawled Bovy Isle."

The notes are very inconsistent and would appear to have been written down on a hurried visit.

With the dissolution of the Monasteries, Tavistock Abbey became Crown property, but the islands are not mentioned in the records. It is clear, however, that the condition of the Islands had degenerated, and although £6,000 had been expended by Edward VI on fortification of which little trace remains, the only use to which they were put—according to a bill of attainder brought against Lord Admiral Seymour in 1549—was as a pirate base; he was accused of entering into relations with pirates "to have gotten into his hands the strong and dangerous isles of Scilly," and "where he might have a safe refuge if anything for his demerits should be attempted against him." For this, and other things, he was convicted and duly beheaded, and the Islands then fell to the Crown as Escheat (5th March, 1549).

STAR CASTLE

Now begins a new era in the history of the islands; the possessions of Lord Admiral Seymour reverted to the Crown in 1549 and the name of Godolphin (Godalghan) first occurs as that of Captain of the Group. William Godolphin and later, Thomas Godolphin, of the famous Cornish family, were military Governors under the Crown until the thirteenth year of Queen Elizabeth; in 1571 Elizabeth leased the islands to Francis, afterwards Sir Francis, Godolphin, for 38 years on condition that he defended them and paid a yearly rental of £10 to the Receiver of the Duchy.* Subsequent leases were granted to the Godolphin-Osborne family at £40 per annum, so that, for some 250 years (except during the Protectorate) they were the owners of the Islands; thereafter, for a further 31 years from 1800, they were leased by the representatives of the Godolphins, the Duke of Leeds, who in 1831 refused to renew the lease.

Shortly after the defeat of the Spanish Armada, in 1588, Queen Elizabeth ordered Star Castle to be built on St. Mary's at the expense of the Crown, partly as a precaution against a further descent from Spain and partly as a protection from pirates and privateers. It should be noted that Don Philip continued to wage war against England long after the defeat of his fleet by Sir Francis Drake. The Spaniards had a base at Brest, from whence issued the four Galleys in 1595 which raided Mousehole and Penzance, and there was good reason to anticipate

*This lease was opposed unsuccessfully by Mr. Edward Barkley, who asserted that Lord Admiral Seymour had purchased only the land held by Danvers, and that he, as residuary legatee of Whittington, was entitled to the castle as a part of the islands that had been wrongfully seized by the Admiral.

that he might use the Scillies;† indeed, if he had assembled his Armada in the Scillies and chosen his weather, history might have taken a different course. It is on record that Philip of Spain instructed his Admiral Menandez, as early as 1574, to seize the Scilly Isles and establish a base there, but fortunately a plague broke out in the fleet, the Admiral died of it, and the scheme was abandoned.

The rendezvous of the Armada was the Scilly Isles, and there are many references in the State papers regarding Spain's intentions regarding the Islands. The following extract from the " General Orders " issued by the Duke of Medina Sidonia at Lisbon to the Armada is of interest :—

" May, 1588 . . . . on leaving Cape Finisterre the course will be to the Scilly Isles, and ships must try to sight the islands from the South, if ships get separated from the Armada they are to continue on the course. If on arrival there the Armada is behind them, they will cruise off the place until the Armada appears . . . "

As a consequence of the Menandez episode, the attention of Elizabeth and her advisers was directed to Scilly, and Francis Godolphin was ordered to conduct an enquiry.

In the Calendar of State Papers (Eliz. I. add: 1579) his reply is given, and some details are of special interest as showing the condition of the isles at that time.‡

(1) The rent of £20 is paid to the Queen for the islands, and she is at no charge, except that she sometimes grants an allowance for powder.

†*Cal. State Papers, Domestic, Elizabeth* 1591, *May*, 17.

" Memorial (by Lord Burghley) for Sir Walter Raleigh to send a pinnace from Plymouth to Lord Thomas (Howard) to warn him of the Spaniards being about Scilly; for Darrell to provide two months' victuals for the Queen's ships, to send Sir Walter Raleigh westward with a commission to take up shipping and men to save Scilly, if not taken, and defend the coasts of Cornwall and Devonshire.

*Quoted from an article by J. E. Hooper in the Journal of the Old Cornwall Society.

Star Castle and Harbour, St. Mary's, from an old print.

Star Castle as it is to-day.

(2) As to Abbey lands, Treskawe Island belonged to Tavistock Abbey, and Chris. Coplestone can shew writings for Brear Island. Mr. Fortescue for Agnes Isles, and the heirs of Mr. Whittington and Mr. Danvers for others. No ancient rents were paid except puffins or like small value.

(3) King Edward VI built two clock houses (Blockhouses) in St. Mary's Isle and began a fort and a house, and two clockhouses of Treskawe, their charge, with that of the garrison, cost £6,000.

(4) Lord Admiral Seymour not only had the Abbey lands, but all the Islands, buying the interests of others.

(5) Since the Islands came into King Edward's possession, 80 tenements have been erected and laborious inclosures of rough land made.

(6) There are now not a hundred men, but more women and children; the tillable ground does not find half of them bread. Only the two islands wherein are fortifications are inhabited; two others are habitable for 20 persons. There are good roads and convenient harbours, and it would be mischievous for the enemy to take them; but I could not defend them in war, without help.

In the Calendar of State Papers appear the following:—

" Aug. 9th, 1587. The Council to Sir George Carey. Report of a fleet of 120 sail having been seen off the Isles of Scilly, supposed to be Spaniards."

' June 23rd, 1588. Information by Sir Francis Godolphin. Of the discovery of the Spanish fleet off the Scilly Islands. Nine sail of great ships between Scilly and Ushant, their sails all crossed over with a red cross. English boats chased and fired at."

"July 6th, 1588. Lord Adm. Howard to Walsygham. . . . Part of the Spanish fleet had been discovered off the Scilly Islands, but had been dispersed by the stormy weather."

In 1593 Queen Elizabeth made up her mind, and Sir Francis Godolphin received the following letter dated 9th May, 1593. "Having resolved upon fortifying St. Mary's Island according to a plan which will be brought to him, order will be given that £400, the estimated charge, be delivered to him of the revenue of that County (Cornwall) as required for keeping such fort and two other sconces. During the summer a lieutenant, three gunners, and twenty-six soldiers are appointed, whose wages will amount to £1 1s. 10d. a day or £30 11s. 4d. a month, but thinks only ten soldiers are necessary in winter.

"He is to see that some of the inhabitants of St. Mary's assist the said retinue if required; has ordered according to his request four iron demi-culverins to be sent, authorises him to send two minions of brass, which are in his custody in Cornwall; he will order powder and bullets for the pieces, and matches, muskets, pikes, and halberds for the Garrison. He is to undertake the building of the fort, with advice of Robert Adams, and to choose the persons to guard it, using circumspection for avoiding superfluous charges.

"Upon knowing from him in what part of Cornwall, next to the Isles, some convenient number may be put in readiness to resort to the Isle upon any great necessity, order shall be given therefor."

The building of Star Castle is a very good and characteristic example of how well Queen Elizabeth was served by her subjects, and how economical, if not mean, was her administration in the matter of rewards. Speed was essential—threatening Spanish vessels were frequently seen near the coast—and Robert Adams must have been a genius, since the whole building commenced in June, 1593, was completed by December, 1594, and not only was the work well and truly done, but he found time to incorporate certain decorations and never for one instant did he fail to preserve those superb proportions that distinguish the best architecture of that period. He received, for his services, 13s. 4d. a day. Up to December, 1594, the cost had reached £958 11s. 2d., of which only £450 had been paid, and although approved at the time, the extra expenditure incurred by Sir Francis was not paid until November 24th, 1603—nine years after its presentation!

The following is taken from the Calendar of State Papers. Domestic—Elizabeth VCCXLV. 72:—

" August 6th, 1593.

> Sir Fras. Godolphin to Lord Burghley. Adams is well deserving, for besides his perfect skill in numbers and measures, he is very provident in saving, and no less painful in attending; the work considered, *so much has seldom been performed at such small charge, and with so few hands, in so short a time.*"

[The italics are ours!]

Star Castle was built on The Hugh, a high rocky peninsular joined to the main part of St. Mary's by a sandy isthmus on which Hugh Town now stands. The stones from Ennor Castle were included in its construction, and the inhabitants of Heyucastle (now Old Town) moved for greater protection as near to the new fortress as possible. The quay at Hugh Town, which was later extended, was built in 1601 and Hugh Town has been the metropolis and port of the Islands ever since.

Star Castle (Stella Mariae) takes its name from the stellar form of the plan; certain of its salients recall the walled cities of Flanders and at the time that it was built, although small, it was rivalled only by Upnor Castle and Tilbury Fort. The two-storied residence, which conforms to the general stellar plan, is surrounded by eighteen-foot granite ramparts on which is a skirting wall with numerous embrasures for muskets and cannon. On the ramparts are four small rooms in each of which a captain of the garrison was lodged, each being privileged to dine at the Governor's table. Over the entrance are the initials E.R. (Elizabeth Regina) and below are R.A. (probably Robert Adams and possibly Sir Ramfrye Arundel) and F.G. (Francis Godolphin). The arched entrance, closed by a portcullis, is surmounted by a bell tower and there is an embrasure for a cannon to command the approach; close alongside is a sally-port. Externally, the castle is surrounded by a dry moat. The Governor's residence (which is now an hotel) contains the original Officers' Mess Room and a massive "Great Kitchen" fireplace, where oxen were roasted whole; below are the dungeons which, during the following century, were used for the confinement of several distinguished political and other prisoners. The original roof was of thatch.

As Carew says: "Sir Francis Godolphin reduced the place to a more defensible plight, and by his invention and purce bettered his plot and allowance, and therein so tempered strength with delight and both with use, as it serveth for a sure Hold and commodious Dwelling."

Calendar of State Papers: Notes by Sir Fras. Godolphin on the importance of keeping the Isles of Scilly:—

"Scilly lies 30 miles from the Land's End of Cornwall W.S.W., being the nearest port of Her Majesty's dominions towards Spain. It is as an inn by which ships trading Westerly or Southerly are to pass and return, whereby it both succours and secures our traffic, and no other place can so aptly permit or restrain the traffic of Ireland and the north of Scotland with France and Spain. The enemy may soon make it impregnable and use it as a rendezvous with his Navy, a citadel or scourge against the realm . . . proving a more hurtful neighbour in the West than Dunkirk is in the East. Neither Falmouth nor Plymouth which have the country's strength always ready to reinforce their garrisons, deserve so strong a guard as Scilly, for those isles cannot be reinforced, being so far distant from the main. In the reign of Her Majesty's brother, they were kept by my father against the French with a guard of 150 men when Falmouth had but 10. I will offer £500 towards the charges needful for the fortifications if Her Majesty would grant me such further term in those Isles as she did to my uncle . . ."

In 1637, it was reported that there were 25 men at Star Castle with 25 more sent from the mainland for six months in the year. The islanders could not muster more than 30 persons able to carry arms.

The first distinguished visitor to Star Castle was Prince Charles, afterwards Charles I, who, together with the Duke of Buckingham and Captain Henry Mainwaring, landed on St. Mary's in September, 1623, and remained for four nights.

The Prince and his suite were on the return journey from Spain, where his prospective marriage (which however did not take place) to the Spanish Infanta, had been discussed. No reason for his landing can be given, but there would appear to have been some discord on board the fleet and the Prince was determined to land.

The following account is taken from the Navy Records:—

"On Sunday, September 21, a Council of War was held on the 'Prince Royal,' at which the possibility of landing the Prince on one of the Isles of Scilly in a ketch was discussed. For this purpose several pilots had put off from the islands, but by the time they reached the flagship, the idea had been postponed. However, after supper the matter was again debated, and beyond expectation, order was given to make ready the longboat and to call the ketch, and the Prince made choice of the company that were to accompany him to the shore.

"About one of the clock after midnight, with great danger to his Highness' person and to the Duke of Buckingham, they were put into our longboat, which was veered astern by a long warp, where the ketch, laying the longboat on board, and the sea going somewhat high, they entered the ketch disorderly, without regard to any, but everyone shifting for himself.

"Being all shipped, the ketch was so overburdened as she could make but little way, so that after we had taken farewell with a discharge of a volley of our great ordinance, we tacked into the sea.

"After six hours' buffeting the ketch succeeded in making St. Mary's Island where the Prince and his retinue landed. The flagship being now for the time bereft of the services of her Captain and also the Master, Walter Whiting, the Earl of Rutland, Commander of the Fleet, held a council on board to decide what course it would be advisable to take. After serious consultation with two pilots of the island it was agreed that the 'Prince Royal' (flagship) might go into the roadstead without danger.

"We came to anchor in the best of the roadstead about two of the clock afternoon, the Prince and all his train standing upon the lower point of the land, and welcomed us in as we passed close by, with much expression of joy and heaving up their hats."

The writer of the above record indicates very clearly that this visit "beyond expectation and involving a stormy and dangerous six hours' voyage in an overburdened ketch at one o'clock in the morning," was not encouraged by the naval experts, but he does not state what motive induced the Prince to visit the Islands in such a hurry and in such an unceremonious manner. On leaving Star Castle the Prince gave Sir Francis Godolphin "a chayne of gold to the value of £50 and many other large giftes."

The family of Godolphin suffered a severe tragedy in October, 1636. The Egmont papers contain the following letter:—"Edmund Percival to Sir Phillip Percival. I advise you to send no cattle over to Ireland whilst the Turks are so busy, lest both your cattle and your gentlemen should suffer, there having been a multitude of passengers taken this summer. Sir Francis Godolphin and his lady, and his servants, and his brother Captain Godolphin and his wife, going to the Isles of Scilly some three or four leagues off the shore, were taken by the Turks, and one of the Turks attempting to abuse the Captain's wife, he presently ran him through whereupon they cut him in a hundred pieces, and they carried Sir Francis and the rest away captives. God of His mercy send us some relief."

In 1635 no less than 20 sail of "Turkish" men-of-war were reported off the Scillies; they were intercepting the fishing fleet on its return from Newfoundland and many complaints are recorded in the State Papers of the period. It is interesting to note that these pirates (Turks, Moors, Algerians, and the Sallee Rovers) were not suppressed until 1816 when Sir Edward Pellew, with English and Dutch ships, bombarded and destroyed the town of Algiers.

The garrison of Scilly in 1642 was 165 men—at a cost of £261 per month.

There are, in existence, fragments of letters written by a Francis Godolphin, of the family of Sir Francis, and probably father of the famous Sydney Godolphin, bearing the date 1643.

"From Francis Godolphin to John Rogers:—

"For your coming over and making up your books, if it were not for displeasing somebody that I never will if I can helpe it, I should be very glad of seeing you, and the place is worth your seeing too; indeed I like it, much better than I did expect, though I must confess I came much the more willingly hither because I was not well at ease where I was . . . There has noe ship come in hither since Jack went, but a Falmouth warrier, which received a broadside from one of the Parl. ships the day before.

"I conceive there can be no possibility of peace. Our God be merciful to us . . . to come hither, considering how glad I am at all hours to have you by me, and the novelty of the place for a few days would entertain you contentedly enough, and more than a few would tire you ten times more than Compton did. There are also some things about this place, I doe not mean the fortification, but the grounds, wherein your judgment, having viewed it, would be of use to me.

"I woud also that you should see my patience, for this place, in respect of an Absolute want of all welcome company, is a strange change to me.

"Yet a very honest man, borne here, may live very happily, as many doe, that would not change for twice soe much a year in Cornwall. For all this, I would by noe means be guilty of drawing you hither if it in any way dislike your best friend. We have seen noe doubtful ship upon the coast a great while. . . .

"I have received a warrant from the King to carry over two hundred men more, for the safeguard of the fort at Scilly for the summer; the estates of divers delinquents, as the Lord Robartes, both Trevills, Bosawen, Sergnt Aubin, and Erisey (?) appointed to be sold . . . out of which £600 is, in the first place, to be paid to me, for provision of a magasin of victualles at Scilly."

In the struggle between Charles I and Parliament, Star Castle once more afforded a refuge for the Cavaliers; in 1646, when the Parliamentarians, under General Fairfax, had defeated the Royalist Army at Bodmin, the Prince of Wales (afterwards Charles II), accompanied by Lord Colpepper and Sir Edward Hyde, left Pendennis Castle and sailed for the Scillies.

The Prince wished to keep his foot on British ground to the last, and sent Lord Colpepper, two days after he landed, to acquaint the Queen (in France) "with the wants and incommodities of the place." Star Castle had been considered a position of great strength, but did not, in this respect, answer their expectations. Lords Capel and Hopton were unable, owing to contrary winds, to sail from St. Michael's Mount to join them for upwards of a month, but when they did they brought a "trumpet" from Fairfax, bearing a letter from Parliament, requesting the Prince to come and "reside in such a place and with such council and attendants as the Parliament should think fit."

The Prince refused and observed "that he had remained in Scilly because he wished to be among his people, but that as in six weeks he had not received more than one day's victual from the mainland, he should be compelled to depart."

On the day after the arrival of the "trumpet" a Parliamentary fleet of twenty-seven ships encompassed the islands, but a heavy gale setting in on that rocky coast, in two hours the vessels all dispersed. In Lady Fanshawe's Memoirs there is an interesting account of her adventures in connection with the Prince's expedition to Scilly. "Five days after, the Prince and all his council embark themselves in a ship called the 'Phoenix' for the Isles of Scilly. They went from the Land's End, and so did we; being accompanied with many gentlemen of that country, among whom was Sir Francis Basset, Governor of the Mount, an honest gentleman, and so were all his family, and in particular we received great civility from them. But we left our house and furniture with Captain Bluett who promised to keep them until such a time as we could dispose of them, but when we sent he said he had been plundered of them, notwithstanding it was well known he lost nothing of his own. At that time this loss went deep with us, for we lost to the value of £200 and more, but, as the proverb says, 'an evil chance seldom comes alone'; we having put all our present estate into two trunks, and carried them aboard with us in a ship commanded by Sir Nicholas Crispe (whose skill and honesty the master and seamen had no opinion of) my husband was forced to appease a mutiny, which his miscarriage caused, and taking out money to pay the seamen, that night following they broke open one of our trunks and took out a bag of £60, and a quantity of gold lace with our best clothes and linen, with all my combs, gloves and ribbons, which amounted to £300 more. The next day, after being pillaged, and extremely sick and big with child, I was set on shore almost dead, in the Island of Scilly. When we had got to our quarters near the castle where the

Prince lay, I went immediately to bed, which was so vile that my footman ever lay in a better, and we but three in the whole house, which consisted of four rooms or rather, partitions, two low rooms and two little lofts with a ladder to go up; in one of these they kept dried fish, which was their trade, and in this my husband's two clerks lay. One there was for my sister, and one for myself, and one amongst the rest of the servants; but when I washed in the morning I was so cold, I knew not what to do, but the daylight discovered that my bed was near swimming in the sea, which the owner told us it never did so but at spring-tide. With this we were destitute of clothes; and meat and fuel for half the Court to serve them a month, was not to be had in the whole Island, and truly we begged our daily bread of God; for we thought every meal our last. The council sent for provisions to France, which served us, but they were bad and little of them; then after three weeks and odd days we set sail for the Isle of Jersey, where we safely arrived, praise be God, beyond the belief of all the beholders from that Island, for the pilot, not knowing the way into the harbour, sailed over the rocks, but being spring-tide, and by chance high water, God be praised, His Highness and all of us come safe ashore through so great a danger."

The Prince remained at Star Castle from 4th March to the 16th April, 1646. The King's Standard, however, floated over Star Castle long after the Prince departed. Sir John Grenville, who had been appointed Governor, held his position there for upwards of five years, the Scillies being the last refuge of the Cavaliers, from whence they fitted out cruisers and harassed all Parliamentary shipping passing to and from the three channels.

The Calendar of State Papers of 1648 reports the proceedings of a Committee of both Houses of Parliament: "To write to the Committee of Cornwall and the Governor of Plymouth and to Sir Hardress Waller, to take care to regain the Island of Scilly before it be further strengthened or the Castle victualed. To notify to Lord General (Fairfax) the revolt of Scilly . . . "

" That the Lord Admiral be acquainted with the revolt of Scilly."

While Sir John Grenville was doing his duty by his king, that monarch was reported to have endeavoured to pledge the Islands as security for a loan of £50,000 from merchants in Amsterdam!

Whitlock, in his Memorials, quotes the following:—

" Letters 26 June 1649, mention that a Frigate of Sir John Granville, Governor of Scilly, with two Bras Guns, 24 Muskets and 24 Oars, coming near Swansea, the Governor of Cardiff sent out Boats, pursued the Frigate from Creek to Creek, and at length took her, and the men, except the Capt. and some few, who got ashore."

" Letters (6 March, 1650) of several ships taken by Pyrates of Scilly and Jersey. Letters of 15 March of the want of Frigates on the Western Coast to keep in the Jersey and Scilly Pirates, and of their taking several Merchantmen, and none of the Parliament Frigates to help them. Letters of 19 March of the Pyracies committed by those of Jersey and Scilly."

Apparently their straits were such that they were forced to commandeer provisions from the ships of any nation passing near enough for the purpose, because, on the plea that Dutch shipping had been seized, Admiral Van Tromp appeared off the islands and demanded satisfaction. Van Tromp's real purpose, however, was to obtain possession of the Islands, and for this purpose he first proposed to hold them for the King against the Parliament and then offered compensation to Sir John Grenville for their surrender, but that faithful officer replied " that it would be inconsistent with his duty to his country to abandon a post, the maintenance of which had been committed to him by his Sovereign." Unable to persuade Sir John to hand over English land to a foreigner, even though Sir John was at war with his own countrymen, Van Tromp sailed away and announced at Plymouth that he had declared war with the Scilly Isles and was ready to proceed with the Parliament against them.

The prospect of a Dutch base on the Scillies, and the clamours of the Merchants who were losing ships and cargoes wholesale, at length attracted the attention of Parliament and an expedition was fitted out under General Blake and Sir George Ascue.

THE SIEGE OF STAR CASTLE

THE Parliamentary fleet set sail from Plymouth, according to Letters quoted in Whitlock's "Memorials":—

17th April, 1651: Letters: "That Lieut.-Col. Clarke with nine Companies of foot, set sail from Plymouth for Scilly Islands."

17th April, 1651: Letters: "That Van Tromp came to Pendennis and related that he had been to Scilly to demand reparation for the Dutch ships and goods taken by them; and receiving no satisfactory answer, he had, according to his Commission, declared war on them."

21st April: "That Van Tromp lay before Scilly and declared that he would assist the English against it."

24th April: Letters: "Of the Fleet's arrival at Scilly and of the guns heard from thence."

26th April: Letters: "That 2,000 of the Parliament's soldiers and seamen were landed in the little Isles on the West of Scilly, and that the Ordnance were heard thundering there many hours together."

2nd May: Letters: "That the Parliament's Fleet at Scilly had taken New Grimsby after 3 times being beaten off, and that they had taken 2 Irish Frigates, one of 30 and the other of 24 guns."

3rd May: "That the Parliamentary soldiers had taken all the Islands except St. Mary's and had taken 3 of their Frigates, killed 14 of their men, and taken 120 prisoners. That of the Parliamentary Forces, 8 were killed and 20 wounded; that they intended to send a summons to St. Mary's Island, and if they refused, then to attempt it."

8th May: "That General Blake and Sir George Ascue with the Fleet at Scilly intend to fall upon St. Mary's Island, that the Governor thereof, Sir John

Greville, sent to them for a Treaty, which was agreed, but took no effect, and thereupon the great guns played upon St. Mary's."

12th May: "Letters from Sir George Ascue of the Action at Scilly, that Captain Morris behaved himself most gallantly in the storming of the Island. That the Scilly Islands are a key that opens a passage to several Nations."

30th May: "That the Foot of Scilly entered at St. Mary's Island, and that those in the Castle were in great want of water."

The following is related by Jos. Leveck in a seventeeth century document, and quoted by "Lanje":—

"We of the Parliament Forces, had laid at sea from Saturday, April 12th, till Thursday, the 17th, when in the morning . . . we put our soldiers in boats to endeavour to make a landing on Tresco; one party was to land in a sandy bay near the Fort at Old Grimsby Harbour, and the other in a more stony bay, somewhat to the westward. We had not reckoned on the strength of the tide, which was on the ebb, and some of our boats were grounded on the rocks and others carried out of their course. So orders were given for all the boats to make straight for Old Grimsby Harbour and we sheltered by a rock in the Channel until we could make a joint attack. We then moved forward, but the pilots and many of the rowers had been taken up in the West Country and were very backward in the service, misguided us, and we came to a little island called Norwithiel, standing in the entrance to the Harbour, and within half-a-musket shot of Tresco. The Pilots swore that it was Tresco, but Captain Bowden was doubtful of it, as none of the enemy came to oppose our landing. Some of the Companies had landed and the boats were aground, but in order that the opportunity might not be lost, the rest of the boats were ordered forward. They were again misguided, and came to a rocky part of Tresco where it was difficult to land. The enemy brought down a body of musketeers, and there was hot firing on our boats from behind rocks on the shore. Our boats were at a disadvantage, being so thickly crammed with men that they could not use their muskets. Here, we endured about 70 great shot beside musketry in abundance, so that many of the boats turned helm and rowed out of range, notwithstanding the struggle of Col. Clarke and other officers. After half-an-hour we all withdrew to Norwithiel, and found that our loss was not so great as was feared. We then rowed to an adjacent Island called Teän, leaving three companies on Norwithiel. We spent a very cold and comfortless night on Teän, and the next day the enemy began firing great shot at us, which fell among our tents but did no great harm. We managed to get some much needed provisions ashore from the ships which were riding at a distance, and we prepared ourselves for a second attempt.

"We sent to Admiral Blake for a better supply of rowers for the boats, and he moreover sent about 200 seamen to attempt the assault with us. We resolved to storm the Enemy by night, and during the day we took careful observations of the Channel and the place of intended landing.

"We drew off our men from Norwithiel in the evening, with the exception of 80 men left to amuse the enemy while we attacked, and about 11 o'clock we set forward. By the mercy of God it was very calm, so that the enemy's frigates could not come up the Channel to do us any harm, although they fired some great shot at us.

"We made fires on Teän to deceive the enemy, and the smoke blew towards Tresco, which somewhat obscured our passage. Yet the enemy discovered us when we were about half way over and fired much ordnance at us, with little hurt.

"The boats came up well together, and though at first forced back, we charged them so resolutely, even with clubbed muskets, that we worsted them, killed 1 captain, 14 men, took prisoners 4 captains and 167 men, the rest fleeing, and none had escaped had we been better acquainted with the Island. We had been opposed by 1,300 men—a greater strength by far than we had imagined.

"Let the exceeding goodness of God to this unthankful nation, in lopping off the bough, even with terror, and giving into our hands a place stuffed with men, a greater number by many than we were, and but yesterday a curse to our Maritime Affairs, a scourge to the Merchants, though invincible for strength, and desperate to attempt with so little loss in so short a time."

The sympathies of the inhabitants can be judged by the feat of a pilot called Nance, who, although "the most knowing pilot of the place," led them to Norwithiel, "affirming on his life" it was Tresco.

When the Parliamentarians had conquered Tresco, General Blake erected an advanced battery to command Broad and Crow Sounds. This battery could reach any ship that went into, or came out from St. Mary's Harbour. In the meantime, Sir George Ascue in the ships, bombarded Star Castle from St. Mary's Sound.

Sir John Grenville soon found his position untenable, since, not only were his ships prevented from approaching the Islands, but the enemy effected a landing on St. Mary's and threw up breastworks and endeavoured to storm the Castle, which was lamentably short of water and provisions of all kinds. It was not, however, until he had sought and obtained permission from his King, then in

Holland, that he consented to surrender on conditions.* It is possible that the conditions were exceptionally favourable because of Sir John's known refusal to treat with Van Tromp, the potential enemy of their common country. The garrison was permitted to march out together with their arms and horses with beat of drums, sound of trumpets, colours displayed and "matches lighted at both ends"—the last of the Cavaliers. They were about 1,500 men, with "enough commissioned officers to head an army." It is not known at what point Van Tromp and his twelve ships left the scene.†

The men were transported to Ireland, Scotland and France, to which countries they probably belonged, while the Governor and some of the chief officers were taken to Plymouth, where Sir John Grenville was soon set at liberty and permitted to embark for the Continent to share the fortunes of his Royal master who, later, created him Earl of Bath: "He attended the King in his greatest distresses, throughout all his disconsolate travels, in France, Flanders, Holland and the Isle of Jersey." There is a Cornish proverb to the effect that "a Godolphin never wanted wit nor a Grenville loyalty." One of the special provisions of the Treaty was that none of the Islanders should suffer, and many Royalist gentlemen remained in Scilly, to await better times, including a representative of the Godolphin family.

The document of surrender was headed as follows:—
*" Articles agreed on this xxiii day of May 1651, by and betweene Admirall Blake and Colonell Clerke, Commanders in chiefe of all the fforces by Sea or Land, in and about the Islands of Triscoe and Briar, of the one part, Sr. John Grenvile, Knight, Governor of the Islands of St. Marye's and Agnes, in Scilly, on the behalfe of his Matie., on the other pt., touching the rendition of the sd. Isles of St. Marye's and Agnes, together with all the Castles, forts, fortresses, sconces and fortifications unto them belonging, to the use and behoof of the Parliam. of England as followeth . . . . . ."

†It is stated in "Cornwall in the Great Civil War," by Miss Mary Coates, that the Islands of Scilly were surrendered to the combined English and Dutch fleets. The Victoria County History, on the other hand, states that Van Tromp appeared off the Islands in March, 1651, with a fleet, demanding reparation for piracies committed on Dutch vessels. The Council of State at once took alarm and made representations to The Hague that Tromp's presence was an unfriendly act and Blake was ordered to take command of Sir George Ayscue's fleet, then ready to sail for the West Indies, fight Tromp if necessary, and not to leave Cornish waters until he had reduced the Isles of Scilly.

Soon after the reduction of the Islands, a strong, circular tower, Oliver Cromwell's Castle, was built to command the Channel between New Grimsby and Bryher and manned by twenty men; a garrison of some 600 men was, for a time, maintained at Star Castle, which provided a very convenient place for political and other prisoners. The first prisoner of note to be confined in the dungeons of Star Castle was Dr. John Bastwick, who had issued a critical pamphlet against Archbishop Laud* and was sentenced by the Star Chamber in 1637 to a fine of £5,000, to be deprived of his ears, to suffer in the pillory and then to be confined in the Scilly Isles. He remained there until 1640. The Duke of Hamilton was entrusted to the care of Sir Francis at Star Castle in 1643. In 1655, John Biddle, the celebrated Socinian (Unitarian) was confined in Star Castle by Oliver Cromwell, to " keep him out of the way of his persecutors." He was allowed a pension of 10s. a week and was released in 1658.

After the surrender to the Commonwealth, Scilly appears to have been neglected, for we find a petition dated May 14th, 1658, from Lt.-Col. Joseph Hunkin, Governor of Scilly, to the Protector: " The stores of ammunition in the garrison are decayed; there are only 77 barrels of powder left here by the enemy at the surrender of the Islands, which is now unfit for service. There is also a great want of Saker and minion shot, there being only two shots apiece for all these guns on the Islands. Begs 200 barrels of powder and three tons of shot so that he may be able to defend the Islands in case of any vicissitude of affairs."

At the Restoration, Charles II sent three prominent Roundheads, Sir John Wildman (the Anabaptist), Sir John Ireton, and Sir Harry Vane, to be confined in the Castle.

*The pamphlet concluded with the following:—
" From plague, pestilence and famine, from bishops, priests and deacons, good Lord deliver us!"

Prince Rupert, in 1649, brought a large number of soldiers from Ireland to aid the garrison, saying " that he would make Scilly a second Venice."

In connection with the Restoration, a memorandum dated March 18th, 1650, is of interest, stating that Sir John and Col. Richard Arundel of Lanherne have written desiring that Sir Richard Grenville might be sent with all speed with 1,000 men and 300 horses, with powder and ammunition and a fortnight's pay, to the Scilly Islands in connection with a plan for a simultaneous rising of the Royalists throughout England, and later Sir Richard writes: " I employed my own monies and great labours in the King's service, as in supplying Sorlingnes (Scilly) with what was in my power."

One further reference to Star Castle as a place of confinement is on record when in 1681 we find that " seven popish priests " were conveyed thither from Newgate.

The only other visitor of note in the seventeenth century was the Grand Duke Cosmo III, in 1669, who left on record in his diary an interesting account of his stay, together with a view of Star Castlé as it then existed; he speaks in terms of praise of the Islands and of his reception, and mentions that the Castle and adjacent batteries were armed with " 130 very beautiful iron culverins " with a garrison of 200 men at a cost to the King of about £4,000 per annum. The fortifications were allowed to fall into decay, but, in the war with Spain in 1740, they were again put into a state of defence and many new batteries were erected on " The Hugh "; the strong entrance gateway and the bastions around the Hugh itself were erected at this period. The gateway bears the date 1742.

The following is a list of the Governors of the Isles bearing Commissions:—

Hon. Sir Francis Godolphin	1593
Hon. Sir William Godolphin	?
Hon. Francis Godolphin	1640
Hon. Sir John Granville (afterwards Earl of Bath)	1651
Lt.-Col. Joseph Himkiss	1658
Hon. Sidney Godolphin	1702
Major Bennett	?
Rt. Hon. Francis Earl of Godolphin ...	1733

Orders—by the Rt. Hon. Francis Earl of Godolphin, Governor and Proprietor of His Majesty's Islands of Scilly.

Orders to be Observed and Obeyed by the Garrison and Islanders.

(1) That in the absence of the Governor and Lt. Governor, the said garrison and islanders do obey the Commanding Officer for the time being, as their Magistrate.

(2) That the islanders on firing of the warning gun do forthwith repair to his Majesty's Star Castle for the defence of the said islands.

(3) That the master gunner and gunners do not presume to go off St. Mary's island without leave from the Commanding Officer for the time being.

(4) That no islander presume to go to the main, without leave from the Commanding Officer for the time being, especially in time of war.

(5) That all pilots make a report immediately to the Commanding Officer for the time being, of all ships they pilot in, with their force, and number of men, and that no pilot presume to carry any ship out without first seeking its clearance from his Majesty's Star Castle.

(6) That all persons who shall land in any of the said islands be forthwith brought before the Commanding Officer for the time being to be examined by him.

(7) That these orders be published in the said islands, and hung up in his Majesty's Star Castle there.

GODOLPHIN.

St. James', 29th May, 1742.

The military establishment was gradually reduced; in 1822 it consisted of a Lieutenant-Governor, a master gunner, four gunners and two or three aged sergeants; in 1857, five invalids (His Majesty's Company of Invalids) manned the fortifications and, finally, in 1863, it was left to the care of one elderly caretaker. In the eighteenth century the salary of the Governor of Scilly Castle and Islands was £1,821 10s., that of the Lt. Governor £731, the master gunner £361 and two other gunners £361 each.

The last military Governors were Lt.-Col. Geo. Vigoureux (immortalised by Sir Arthur Quiller Couch in his story "Major Vigoureux") and Major-General J. N. Smyth, who died in Scilly in 1838.

The Scilly archipelago, owing to its position at the mouth of the three channels, assumes importance in any war or threat of war involving Great Britain, within recent times the Government have considered making a naval base of Scilly, and new batteries were constructed at a cost of a quarter of a million pounds as late as 1905, but these batteries were never, in fact, mounted and, in the first Great War, a naval base and flying boat base were centred here, with approximately a thousand men.

In the second world war the Islands were heavily defended and formed an important air and sea base in the Battle of the Atlantic.

THE SCILLONIANS

THE inhabitants of these Islands seemed to have been ignored in the midst of the stirring events that took place on their homelands and, in fact, we know very little about them up to the sixteenth century; the Scillies are not mentioned in Domesday Book. We have very good evidence, in the form of prehistoric remains, that the Islands were inhabited by people of the Early Bronze Age, some 4,000 years ago. Under several feet of soil, notably at Bant's Carn, St. Mary's, and on St. Agnes, the erosion of the sea has disclosed rude round stone huts and, from the surrounding middens or refuse heaps, fragments of pottery, similar to that found in the barrows, have come to light, showing that they date from the same period. In addition to pottery fragments, bones of horse, sheep and a small kind of deer, together with stone, flint and bone tools, stone querns for grinding corn, and innumerable shells of limpets (one of the stable articles of diet on the sea coast in those days) have been unearthed; flint scrapers for dressing skins of animals, awls and whorls and spindles for weaving garments, stone mace-heads and flint arrow-heads have been collected in great quantity.

There is little doubt that these early settlers were hunters, fishermen, farmers and sailors and that their food consisted of meat, grain and fish; they were, no doubt, well able to defend themselves against aggression and it is probable that the ancient cliff fort at Giant's Castle, St. Mary's, was one of their defensive points. It is known that these early bronze age people developed a high degree of organisation and were intrepid sailors, who roamed the seaboard from Gibraltar to the Shetlands and Scandinavia, and communicated freely with their compatriots in Gaul, Ireland and elsewhere.

View from the Old Quay, St. Mary's. *Photo : Gibson, Scilly.*

Daffodils, St. Mary's. *Photo : Gibson, Scilly.*

The successive races and tribes that are said to have inhabited Britain, and probably the Scillies, commence with the Turanian, a primeval race of which the Basque and Finns are kin, followed by the Iranian who spoke an intermediate language between Egyptian and Sanscrit, which we term Celtic.

The Iranians, according to the legend, occupied Britain in three successive tribes, the Alwani, after whom the country was called Albion, the Aedui, whence Eiddyn (Edinburgh), and the Britons, who named the Island Britain, from their god Bryt (or Pryt) and " ain," an island.

The Celts were also called Galli or Gaels (followers), either from their clannish habits or from their nomadic mode of life, and they were the race of whom the Druids were priests. The functions of the Druids were, so it is stated, religious and judicial, and they were the superiors of the entire body. The next order was that of the bards or poets, who were required to commit to memory some twenty thousand verses of Druidical dogmata and to educate the young. The lowest order was that of the vates, who predicted events and used enchantments. The Celts of the South-West district appear to have borne a name of which Corn was the commencement, perhaps referring to the " horn " of land that they occupied. They were later called the West Wealas, but this must have been by the Saxons, " Welsh " being an offensive appellation, signifying an unintelligible stranger.

The derivation of the name Scilly cannot be stated with any certainty, nor can the fact that the small rock of that name should have given the name to the whole archipelago (if indeed it did) be explained.

The following are names given to the islands:—

Hesperides ... ... The Fortunate Islands or Western Islands

Cassiterides ... ... Tin Islands
Sigdeles
Sillinae, Silures, Sylina or Silia ... ... Roman
Sylly, Sylley (or Syley)
Sulley (Sully) (from Sul (sun) and ey (island)?
Sulleh (flat rocks dedicated to the sun) ... Briton
Sylleh
Mictis (Timaeus) possible identification with Scilly.
Lissia? (Antoninus)
Sillane (Carew)
Sylinancis
Sillines
Syllingar
Svilla. Hereford Mappa Mundi (1275)
Oestrymnides ... ... Festus Avienus
Sorlings ... ...Dutch
Sorlinges ... ... French
Syllingerne ... ... Norse
Sylla ... ... William of Worcester
Surluse (or Surluce) ... ... Malory
The Long Isles (?) ... ... Malory
Sullee Woodley suggests may be from Greek word " Sullee," signifying to plow, or dig, or gather (tin)
Our Isles ... ... Old grants
Syllye ... ... William of Worcester
Ynis (island)
Essyllwg* Native name said to have been corrupted by Romans to Silures

It has been suggested that the name is derived from the German " selig " (blest) and again that the ancient pronunciation was Skilly (cut off), meaning the scattered islands.

*The celebrated Caractacus commanded men of Essyllwg: they were defeated in A.D. 50.

The most popular theory, however, is that the name comes from " Silya " or " Selli," the Cornish for " conger eel," but some believe that it came from Scylla, associated with the Scylla and Charybdis of Italy and Sicily whose situation is, in some respects, not dissimilar with Britain and the Islands; others maintain that the name is a natural outcome of the use of the word " insulae " (islands) which became contracted to " sulae " or " Sully "—as it is spelt in old documents—and thence to Scilly by a slight misreading of the letter " u."

A mere misplaced dot, perhaps!

Scillonians have been sensitive to the implications of the pronunciation " silly "—even in the eighteenth century they were protesting, on that account, their innate wisdom—it was, we think, Queen Elizabeth who said that " the further West she travelled within her dominions the more sure she was that the wise men came from the East (!) However that may be, it is preferable to say " the Isles of Scilly " rather than "the Scilly Islands."

To sum up, it would seem that etymologically speaking, if we had to give a name to these islands, all our researches in different directions would coincide, inevitably, in the cognomen " Scilly "!

The Isles have had their ups and downs, not only in their politics, but in their social and economic conditions.

Starting from somewhere between 2500 and 2000 B.C., when the sea-borne culture of the East reached them from the Mediterranean and perhaps from Britanny, to the end of the Early Bronze Age, 1400 B.C., they would seem to have been, with Cornwall, an entrepôt for the gold trade between Ireland, the South of Spain and the Eastern Mediterranean; in the Middle Bronze Age, 1400-1000 B.C., however, this trade, according to Hencken, began to take an overland course, through England and Northern Europe to the head of the Adriatic, and the South-West of England suffered a decline due to the collapse of sea traffic. In the late Bronze Age, 1000-350 B.C., much of this traffic reverted to the sea and to South-Western Britain, and it was in this period that tin mining flourished although the beginnings of the trade may have been as far back as 2000 B.C.

There is evidence that from the Early Bronze Age to the Roman occupation (with a possible break between 1400-1000 B.C., that South-Western Britain and the Islands were relatively densely populated, and we believe that the main source of income at this period was tin. The discovery, at about the commencement of the Christian era, of tin in other places, notably Spain, caused a further decline until it revived again in the Middle Ages and continued without a break until 1918. The Islands can have taken little if any part in this trade after the Roman occupation, *circa* A.D. 50.

The earliest invaders were Iberians, short people, dark haired and complexioned, traces of which are said to survive to the present day in Cornwall and Scilly; these were followed by successive waves, from the 6th century B.C. onwards, of Celts, fair-haired, blue-eyed and tall, whose religion was Druidism. The aboriginal, doubtless, was harried by the Saxon, the Saxon by the Dane, and the Dane by the Norman—all kinsmen of the great Indo-Germanic race.

The evidence of Druidism in Scilly is very uncertain; the antiquarian Borlaze professed to find innumerable sacrificial stones, but the natural action of the elements on granite in the islands is so bizarre that human agency must always be doubted. Troutbeck and Borlaze attribute the rock basins on Scilly to the sacrificial rites of Druidism,

Gilbert calls them "supposed relics"; North considers them the work of chance; and Whitfield, on the same subject, reminds us of a story: "Here," quoth Montbarns, waxing eloquent as he described to a guest the imaginary Roman camp, "here was the Praetorian Gate." "Praetorian here, praetorian there," replied Edie Ochiltree, "I mind well the diggin o't!"

Communications between Gaul, Ireland, Cornwall and the Scillies must have been established at a very early date, long before the Roman occupation. After the Romans had left Britain, the Scandinavian Northmen used the Scillies as a base, but have left us no material evidence of their stay; the Saxons arrived perhaps with Athelstan, and thereafter the population, except for a break in the seventeenth century, followed the normal course applicable to the mainland.

What evidence has been produced, and what little archaeological work has been done, goes to show that the islands supported a large population, and suggests that the greater part must have been on land now covered by the sea.

The first named Celtic speaking tribe to inhabit the islands were the Dammonii, a tribe that spread itself over Somerset (to the Mendips), Dorset, Devon, Cornwall and South Wales. The Cornish Dammonii colonised Armorica (Brittany) about the fifth century A.D., and the Bretons and Cornish are relics of the "Celtic Fringe." Henry Jenner tells us that when he visited Brittany he was regarded as a compatriot, and that though political loyalties are very strongly aligned to England and France respectively, to a Cornishman an Englishman is a "foreigner," and so is a Frenchman to a Breton!

Strabo describes the inhabitants of the Scillies as wearing a dress similar to that of the people of the South of Spain, a black mantle sagum or loena. The descendants of these Iberians probably mixed with successive waves of West Britons, Saxons, Northmen and odd emigrants from Scotland, Ireland, Gaul and the Mediterranean; the situation of the Islands would make it possible for a great variety of sojourners, some of whom may have remained. Up to the 16th century we know little beyond the fact that the inhabitants were Christians and agriculturalists; no monuments or commemorative buildings or articles have been preserved of later than Bronze Age relics, other than a Roman altar and the ruins of St. Helen's Church and St. Nicholas' Abbey.

Eustathius calls the natives of Scilly "Melancholi" because of their habit of wearing black clothing down to their ankles; Solinus says that "they lived according to their old manner; they had no markets, nor did money pass among them; but they gave in exchange one thing for another, and so provided themselves with necessaries; they were very religious, both men and women, and pretended to have great skill in the Art of Divination, or in foretelling of what was to come. And as to the healthful state of their climate, Sardus was persuaded that they lived so long till they were weary of life; because they threw themselves from a Rock into the Sea, in hopes of a better life."

Camden states, of that time (1586), that: "The inhabitants are all newcomers, but remains show much previous habitation." This presents one of the mysteries connected with the Islands and one which may never be solved; one may speculate exhaustively as to the reason why a total population should have deserted the Islands and then be replaced with newcomers. It may, of course, have been due to some convulsion of nature, such as an inundation of land that would cause a widespread sense of insecurity and consequent emigration; it may have been due to some pestilence or to a raid that might have annihilated them; or merely to hard living and the prospect of better subsistence elsewhere; it is possible, also, that the "newcomers" made a clean sweep of the existing peoples, but historical records do not help us in any way. It may be taken for granted, however, that none of the Scillonians of the present day claim descent from inhabitants of the Islands before the 16th Century. It is probable that the earliest settlers that provide a connecting link with present day families were squatters; some are known to have come from Scotland and Ireland, and no doubt Cornwall contributed its share. Many of the existing families of Scillonians, or of Scillonians who were until recently resident in the Isles, trace their descent from the Godolphins; the Edwards, the Crudges, the MacFarlands, Mumfords, Banfields and Tregarthens are all connected with the Godolphin family through the marriage of Ursula, a daughter of Sir Francis Godolphin, to John Crudge, of Scilly.

There is no doubt that the popularity of the early Godolphins resulted in a number of families leaving Cornwall for the Scillies, and it is probable that this influx of highly favoured mainlanders completely dominated the previous inhabitants, who, at that period, must have lived at a very low subsistence level.

There is a story of an inhabitant of Bryher, employed on the construction of the fortifications on "The Hugh," St. Mary's, who rowed himself daily backwards and forwards across the two miles or so of sea and received, for his no doubt long and arduous labours, the princely sum of 6d. a week!

Since at various times a large garrison of soldiers has been kept on the Islands, including Grenadier Guards and a Company of the Bedford Regiment—that, tradition has it, were forgotten and left to fend for themselves on the Islands—it is certain that a good deal of inter-marriage resulted, and no doubt many time-expired men, whose wives had relations on the Isles, settled there. In 1669, Duke Cosmo III reports on his visit to the Isles: " Corn of late began to be scarce, in consequence of the increase of the population produced by marriages of the soldiers of the garrison with the islanders, but this has been remedied for some years past by forbidding them to marry! "

Each island has a generic nickname, which is still occasionally in use, but rapidly dying out. St. Mary's men are Bulldogs, Tresco men are Caterpillars (probably associated with smuggling and files of keg-carriers as seen in the moonlight).

Bryher men are Thorns, or " lop-sided " or " one-sided." It is frequently averred that whatever is done by the men of Bryher is aslant, that they walk slightly askew, carry their heads slightly bent sideways, hold a cup or glass at an angle, and generally appear " one-sided."

St. Martin's men are Ginnicks (etymology unknown).

St. Agnes' men are Turks (probably some association with Algerian pirates—often called Turks).

There are certain characteristics which used to distinguish the inhabitants of the different islands and which in some cases are still noticeable, but the motor-boat has served to do what the bicycle has done for the mainland villages, and there is constant and daily intercommunication between one island and another, so that the young men have no difficulty in finding wives from islands other than their own; moreover, all the Islanders are inveterate travellers and think nothing of journeys to, as they put it, England.

The last two wars resulted in a great number of men joining the Services, and in particular the Merchant Navy, and many Service men, stationed on the Islands, have married Scillonians. St. Mary's people have always been cosmopolitan and St. Martin's people the most dependent on themselves. St. Martin's was supposed to have been peopled mainly from Sennen, in Cornwall, and although exclusive, they are said to co-operate well amongst themselves; many show Scandinavian blood and tend to red-headedness; they are very hard workers and their women have high, shrill voices, so that it is said that when a St. Martin's boat reaches Hugh Town Quay the people of Porthcressa Bay know that they have arrived! North says that they were tall and thin. St. Agnes' men are mainly short and thick, with dark hair and eyes, and their speech is short and crisp; in the nineteenth century many of the farmers were pilots who boarded the passing ships and piloted them to their mainland ports. They were said to have long silken beards.

Bryher men are noted as excellent fishermen, and it used to be remarked that Bryher people were quarrelsome and could not co-operate together in any undertaking.

Tresco people, according to North, are of intermediate stature between those of St. Martin's and St. Agnes'.

St. Mary's people have no peculiarities of their own. Their main family surnames used to alternate between Banfields, Edwardes, Tregarthens, Bluets, Gibsons and Mumfords. Certain surnames still predominate on the "Off" Islands, but this is less noticeable nowadays: St. Agnes has several families named Hicks and Legge; Tresco, Bryher and St. Martin's have Jenkins, Pender, Ashford or Ellis.

The Society for the Promotion of Christian Knowledge maintained schools, but education was established by Augustus Smith, the Lord Proprietor, on what amounted to a compulsory basis and was in most cases free. This existed some two generations before compulsory free education was introduced into the mainland. According to North, in 1850 the children were receiving instruction in "all that is requisite for their station in society"!

Notwithstanding this limited curriculum, Scillonians distinguished themselves in all walks of life and continue to do so in the professions in England, and in the mechanical or scientific fields or in the Services, both there and in all corners of the world.

Of their speech, it may be said that it shows less idiom, and more nearly approximates to English as spoken by the educated, than any rural county on the mainland, and this without the slightest affectation. It may well be due to the teachers chosen by Augustus Smith in the middle of the nineteenth century. Woodley (1822) observes that, even in his time, " their mode of pronunciation is very pleasing to an accurate ear," though he notes the dropping of the " h " from the compound consonants " thr "; thus they call three " tree," throat " troat," and pronounce " i " as though it were " oi," thus: pie, " poy "; line, " loin." This is not now noticeable.

Woodley states that Tresco and Bryher had more of a Cornish pronunciation and that St. Mary's and St. Martin's spoke the best English, though what the " best English " may be is a controversial subject, and there may well be some truth in the observation that " the best English is spoken in Vienna "—where they take the trouble to learn it!

In the early days, from the time of Athelstan onwards, the Scillonians must have been industrious, tilling the soil, battling with the special enemies of agriculture on Scilly, the strong winds and burning salt spray, yet none of this would appear to have been worth a comment by those who have left us our fragmentary records, although the punishment of wrongdoers was " news " and thus has received a quite unfair measure of publicity.

We have noted the punishment for felons in Edward I's time. The Crown leases conferred on the lessees conclusive jurisdiction in all plaints and causes—heresies, treasons, matters of life and limb and Admiralty questions excepted. Until the reign of George IV (1827) the clerical order (as on the mainland) had benefit of clergy and were exempt from civil punishment.

The lessee, who was termed the Lord Proprietor, created a "Court of Twelve" to administer local affairs, and this court, by virtue of its isolation and situation and the absence of the Lessee, soon assumed dictatorial powers. At one time we find them issuing an order prohibiting masters of vessels from importing strangers, or exporting residents, under a penalty of £10; at another time a troublesome thief is ordered to be put on board the first of his Majesty's ships of war that might call; women were ducked at the Quay-head; men and women were ordered to be publicly whipped. Paupers were deported to the Mainland and the population restricted to the prevailing economic conditions. Towards the end of the eighteenth century a man of St. Agnes was charged with Sabbath-breaking by digging potatoes, but owing to his extreme poverty the case was dismissed on the delinquent promising "not to do it again"; a woman on St. Mary's was sentenced to receive 50 lashes on the bare back for stealing a cotton shirt.

Borlaze says, however, that in his time, 1756, they (the Court of Twelve) "meet once a month, hear complaints, and compose some little disputes, but rather by compromise than decision, and this is all the government they have, without calling in the Military Power . . . common immoralities escape all reprehension . . . so that the people are left too much to their own will (happy effects of liberty without law!), and as the Islands have but the Shadow of Government, the Good feel not the benefit of it because 'tis but a shadow, nor the wicked the weight of it for the same reason."

Heath, an officer of the Garrison, who wrote in 1750, and must have been a wit, says:

" The spiritual court of Scilly is the ' ducking chair ' at the quayhead, into which offenders in language or morality are put by order of the ' Court of Twelve,' and receive their purification in salt or holy water. The punishments in Scilly are fines, whipping or ducking. There is no prison for the confinement of offenders, which shows that the people are upright enough not to require any, or that the place is a confinement in itself. No venomous insects or reptiles or attorneys or sheriff's officers are ever harboured in these islands."

He enumerates the trades exercised in Hugh Town in his time: bakers, brewers, coopers, butchers, weavers, tailors, mantua-makers, shoe-makers, sail-makers, joiners, carpenters, masons, smiths and perriwig-makers.

Islanders, by the nature of their situation, develop an ability to master all trades, and it is not surprising that the Scillonians have weathered many economic " blizzards " by the simple process of changing their means of livelihood.

There is no authentic evidence which could convict the inhabitants either of deliberate wrecking of ships or of smuggling in olden days, but there can be little doubt that, up to the time of the use of lighthouses, the islands obtained a regular harvest from wrecks, and that smuggling was by no means unknown.

In 1684 the making of Kelp, an alkali of value to glass-makers, soap-makers and bleachers, was commenced, and immense quantities of seaweed were collected and burnt in kilns; this industry continued for some hundred and fifty years and became one of the mainstays of their economic life. There was also a certain amount of weaving and long-line fishing for ling, a good deal of which was dried, salted and exported. Scilly ling was famous.

Lord Nelson wrote from Toulon to a friend in Plymouth, in October, 1803, thanking him for a present of Scilly ling, " which he had much enjoyed."

During and after the Napoleonic Wars (1805-1814) there was widespread distress in the Islands and particularly in the " Off " Islands, and the findings of a Deputation sent by the Penzance magistrates in 1819 give a good illustration of the activities of previous years. The causes of distress in the " Off " Islands, according to the report, were tabulated as follows:

" (1) To the bad harvests of the two preceding years.

" (2) To the failure during the preceding year of the means of making kelp.

" (3) To the decrease of employment in piloting resulting from the establishment of branch pilots, by which employment was monopolised by very few hands.

" (4) To the failure in a considerable degree of the ling fishery.

" (5) To the entire suppression of smuggling by the Preventive boat system, by the loss of which contraband trade the Islanders lost their chief means of support."

In consequent of this Report and its publication in the " Times " and other London newspapers, a General Committee was formed and subscriptions invited. No less than £9,000 was collected, a sum that was administered by a Resident Agent for the Committee, and used mainly in an attempt to establish a pilchard and mackerel fishery by means of the purchase of suitable boats, the rehabilitation of the existing ones and the erection of storehouses.

Unfortunately, either owing to misdirection of this enterprise, or maladministration, or possibly to the vagaries of the pilchard (who is somewhat unreliable in his habits), the expected alleviation of conditions did not take place, and the distress continued for some years. Or, as the proverb has it:

" SCADS and TATIES all the week
AND conger-pies on Sundays."

In due course the Islands recovered their prosperity by their own unaided efforts.

The population has not varied greatly in the last few centuries; the five larger islands are inhabited, and the Island of Samson, which supported at one time some forty or fifty inhabitants, was finally evacuated in 1859 owing to the poorness of the living and to the difficulty of administering the older people there; nineteen men and boys from Samson lost their lives in the shipwreck of a French barque that they had captured during the Napoleonic Wars and which struck on the Wolf Rock when they were taking her as a prize to Devonport. The Island never recovered from this disaster. Several of the smaller islands show traces of occupation in remote times and, in the height of the kelp-making period, some of them, notably Teän, were for a time reoccupied. In the nineteenth century the early potato trade was for many years of great benefit to the islanders, as the soil on all the islands and the climate were particularly suitable for their culture.

Robert Heath, in his " Account " of the Islands and general account of Cornwall dated 1750, gives a description of Cornish wrestling which, so he says, may have been introduced by Corineus, who, wrestling with the Giant Gogmagog at Plymouth, threw him over the cliff and was given Cornwall as a reward; on the other hand, we suggest, it might equally well have been introduced by the Tyrian Hercules, who was said to have visited the Tin Islands and whose epithet was " PALAEMON," the

Wrestler. Heath's account is full of quaint conceits and language which sounds strange in these days; he speaks of the "Manly Sports" and "Whimsical Diversions" of his time, and his description of Cornish hurling is not only interesting as showing what we think must be the genesis of the game of Rugby, but also as an indication of what manner of men they were in the seventeenth and eighteenth centuries. Here then is the "Whimsical Diversion" of hurling in his own words and based on those of Richard Carew in his "Survey" (1602).

"Hurling—Exercises are denominated from hurling or casting a ball. In hurling to Goals, fifteen, twenty or thirty players, more or less, chosen on a Side, strip and join hands, one rank against another; from these ranks they match by pairs, every of which couple, after distributing themselves, are duly to observe each other in time of play. Two bushes are pitched in the Ground about eight or ten feet asunder, directly against which, at the distance of ten or twelve score yards, are pitched two more bushes, in like manner, which are called the goals, appointed by lots to the respective adverse parties. A couple of the best stopping Hurlers, on each side, are placed before each of the two goals for a guard; the rest of the Hurlers, on both sides, are distributed about in the midst, betwixt both goals; when, a ball being thrown up, whoever can catch it, and convey it between the bushes of the adversary's goal wins the game. But one player is no sooner possessed of the ball than another endeavours to seize him, who now strikes his adversary hard on the breast with his doubled fist, called butting, to keep him off, which, if smartly done, is deemed a notable piece of manhood.

"If the catcher defeats the first onset he is taken in hand by another, and so by a third, till he casts the ball from him, called dealing, to one of his partners, who, catching the same, runs with it for the Goal, as before, and if, by his activity, he shakes off or outruns his next adversary, he finds a fresh man or two, near the goal, ready to give him a repulse; and therefore it is by a very unequal Match, or accidents extraordinary, when many goals are won or lost. However, that side carries away the most reputation that gives the most falls in the hurling, keeps the ball longest, and presses the adversary nearest to his own goal.

" Sometimes it is agreed that one chosen person of each side deals the Ball.

" The Hurlers to Goals are bound to observe these Orders, or Laws:

" (1) To hurl man to man, and not two to oppose one man at once.

" (2) In contending for the ball, if a man's body touches the Ground, or the like, and he cries ' Hold ' (which is a word of yielding) and delivers the ball, he is not to be further pressed.

" (3) The Hurler against the ball must not butt, nor hand-fast under girdle.

" (4) That he who has the ball must butt only in his opponent's breast.

" (5) That the Hurler must deal no foreball, or throw it to any partner standing nearer the goal than himself.

" (6) In dealing the ball, if any of the adverse party can catch it flying, or before it is seized fast by the Party dealing it, the property of it is thereby transferred to the catching party; and so the assailants become defendants, and defendants assailants.

" A Breach made in any of these Articles is motive sufficient for the Hurlers going together by the Ears, with their fists. Nor do any seek to take Revenge but in the same manner,

" These Hurling Matches are chiefly used at Weddings, where the Guests commonly undertake to encounter All Comers."

Certainly a " Whimsical Diversion " ! Note the " forward throw," the " mark," and finally the " scrum " —going together by the ears !

Heath does not describe the ball, which was of cork or applewood coated with silver, but says :

" The ball, in this kind of exercise, is endowed with a kind of Magic Property; for whoever catches it becomes immedately like a Mad-man; fighting and struggling with those who go about to hold him; and no sooner has the ball left him, but his Fury goes with it to another, and he becomes immediately peaceable and calm himself."

He adds : " . . . you shall see the Hurlers retire, as from a pitch'd Battle, with bloody noses, wounds and bruises, and some with broken and disjointed limbs, which are all deemed fair play, without even consulting an Attorney, Coroner, or petty lawyer about the Matter."

At this stage, presumably, they got on with the Wedding !

Heath further comments : " Though these bold, active and manly Exercises may be looked upon as pernicious, in beholding the particular hurts, as yet, they are productive of Courage, Worth and Bravery among a people, they should by all means be encouraged, especially in a nation famed for glorious Exploits, among its foreign and effeminate Neighbours."

LOCAL CUSTOMS

In these days of ruthless realism and machines, while education remains subordinate to the immediate requirements of modern social and political economy, there is little room left for the imagination. In the rigorous elimination of superstition, not only have we lost the bad, but all the impetus to imagery and poetry that went with it—and we have nothing to replace it.

One by one our customs and folk-lore have disappeared, and we individuals are left with nothing but our own private superstitions, of the order of spilling salt and the number thirteen, etc., and a disposition to regard " old wives' tales " as utterly beneath notice. Our fairy tales have been murdered by the internal combustion engine (to no particular purpose, for spiritual values do not seem to have been enhanced thereby), and we have only set up a monstrous bogey of economic distress, for the much more colourful witch or sorcerer and his occasionally baneful supernatural powers.

One would expect to find a trace of Celtic fancy surviving in the Islands, but nothing of this is nowadays encouraged (no doubt for excellent reasons) by the schools. Legends, other than that of Lyonesse, are dim; the best known is the legend of a prison and nunnery at Le Val (Holy Vale) and that of the Hermit of St. Helen's mentioned in the chapter on the Vikings. Others are mostly the creation of writers of the nineteenth century and must be classed as fiction.

Amongst the customs that survived until quite recent times, and which we hope will be revived, was the crowning of the May Queen on May Day and the erection of the maypole on the " Parade " in the centre of Hugh Town. The Queen processed round the town, the streets of which were littered with millions of yellow gorse petals which had been gathered by the children for the occasion. May whistles, cut from alder or sycamore branches, and the blowing of cowhorns added to the merriment.

An annual Fair was held on the Green of Hugh Town on Whit-Mondays. Midsummer night was "tar-barrel night," when blazing torches were carried and bonfires set alight. Harvest Festivals were prodigious affairs. The Harvest Festival was called "Nicla Thies," and occurred when the last grain had been gathered. On the near approach of Christmas, the goose-dancers (a survival of the Morris-dancers), merry maskers or guise-dancers, made their appearance. Maidens would dress up as men, sometimes in ship captains' uniforms and the men would dress up as maidens, and they would proceed to dance about the streets; some of the men and women would go in party-coloured dress, half of one colour to the right and left, or above and below, says Heath, while the children would blacken their faces and don hideous masks and parade with them.

The custom of going "limpeting" on Good Friday, according to Jessie Mothersole, still continued in 1914, but limpets have no attraction for the islanders nowadays and shrimping has taken its place. Young and old used to make a point of making and releasing paper boats on the water on Good Friday. The origin of this custom is unknown, and it may well be a votive offering to the sea.*

The Shrove Tuesday custom of throwing stones in the evening against the doors of dwelling houses, until bought off with pancakes or money, has been mentioned in the chapter on Tin.

*The only guess that we can make is that it is a survival from Viking visitations: Friday, the Scandinavian FRTG-DOEG, was regarded as the luckiest day of the week. Perhaps the paper boats represent symbolically the various enterprises to be engaged in during the succeeding year and are an invitation to the gods to take notice and to prosper them.

On 5th November the boys of St. Mary's had a holiday called "Ringing Tide," part of which day they spent in ringing the church bells.

Of legends, that of the so-called "Saint" Warna is the most persistent. St. Warna was supposed to be an Irish saint who landed in a coracle on St. Warna's Bay, St. Agnes, and possessed the power of attracting ships to their doom. The St. Agnes' people were said to propitiate the "Saint" and invoke her aid during poor wrecking seasons (!) by dropping pins into her "Well" on the day after Twelfth Day. Others claim that St. Warna's Bay is a corruption of "Santa Juana," a Spanish ship said to have been wrecked there.

There are a few proverbs, quoted by Jessie Mothersole:

"Southerly wind and fog
Easterly wind all snug."

and

"You may look for six weeks of weather in March."

Of fancies, it is said that a cat lying in front of the fire with its tail turned to the North is an indication of a gale of wind. The granite in Hugh Town is claimed to possess the property of glistening early in the morning in advance of fine weather, whereas when it is dull, a storm may be expected.

Here is a "grace" said before a Scillonian wedding feast by the brother of the bride while the guests were impatiently waiting to commence:

"One word is as good as ten
Eat away—Amen!"

Weddings were formerly the occasion for great feasts which were kept up all day and most of the night, and ended only with the final "bride's dance."

Dancing is frequently mentioned in the record, but only one seems to have any local flavour, which it shares with West Cornwall, the Phoebe (Phoebe was the Moon Goddess) or Phibbie:

" Cannot you dance the Phoebe,
Don't you see how my shoulders shake,
Don't you see what pains I take,
Cannot you dance the Phoebe? "

Perhaps, after all, our modern dances are not so new!

Of superstition, we are informed by Whitfield (1852) that Tresco " swarmed " with witches, and Heath (1750) says that it cannot be expected that these islands should be quite free of Delusions. " Some few here imagine (but mostly old women) that women with child, and the first born, are exempted from the power of witchcraft; and tell you a story of a bewitching woman, that bewitched a man with blindness, who refused her a pin . . . fairies are said to have frequented Buzza Hill on St. Mary's Island, but their nightly Pranks, aerial Gambols and Cockle-Shell Abodes are now quite unknown. Haunted Houses, Giants and Apparitions (so terrible in Scilly some years ago) are now, by application made to the Knowing Men of Cornwall, all charm'd, cast in a Spell, or conjur'd out of the Islands."

A most businesslike way of dealing with the situation!

Of medical practice in his time, says Heath: " For want of Male practitioners in Physic, the few diseases and hurts in these healthful Islands have, for these many years past, been remedied by a ' Society of Skilful Aunts,' constituting a sort of College of Physicians in Scilly, of which Aunt Sarah is the Head or President . . . . When they assemble upon a woeful, desperate or doubtful case, they resign the patient to God and Nature, while the attending Doctress provides a warm room, a nurse, and fit necessaries, which co-operate with uncommon success. Common diseases here (not proceeding from Luxury, Laziness and Intemperance) are cured by one of the subordinate practitioners with a few Simples, without calling in the assistance and judgment of a second or third graduate.

" They have some disguised Nostrums and Specificks, the true Secrets of which Compositions are deposited with their President . . . Mrs. Sarah Jenkins (commonly called Aunt Sarah) . . . a person of singular skill and circumstance, she does many acts of charity and benevolence to the poor-distressed; to which the rest of the younger sisterhood, who are not a little amiable, contribute their parts. The president is remarkable for her venerable long beard, which some imagine operates miraculously to the Benefit of those who stroke it." (!)

We have quoted from Heath extensively since he was the first chronicler to pay any special attention to the Scillonian people as such, excusing himself by saying: " I consider that the little oddities in the customs and manners of the lower class of people are not without amusement and instruction; " " Here," says he, " truth appears in its natural simplicity, unadorned with meretricious embellishments, and beautiful in its own nakedness. Honour, Justice and every social virtue is exercised among them in the strictest punctuality, though there is never a lawyer and but one clergyman, in all the Islands."

After Heath's time, there were a succession of clergymen who wrote accounts of the Islands; the Rev. John Troutbeck (1794) was followed by the Rev. G. Woodley (1822). Woodley commences by soundly rating Troutbeck and Heath for many pages, summarising Heath by saying: " In a word, Heath's Account may be read once for curiosity but will never be referred to with pleasure."

It can be said of Heath, however, that he had humour and a tolerance for the foibles of the islanders, whereas it is evident from his writings that Woodley had little understanding and no appreciation of their independent outlook on life. His stay must have been profoundly unhappy.

Of the products of the soil Woodley tells us that wheat, barley, pillas and potatoes were grown—pillas was a kind of wheat without husk—and of the cattle, he says that they were black and small which, in the " Off " Islands, are fed in a great measure on seaweed! Horses, he adds, are small and generally poor, " their chief food is the furze which they find on the hills, and which they carefully bruise with the fore-hoof before manducation; yet I have been assured that both cows and horses, by custom, acquire such a relish for these peculiar and piquant articles of food, that they pine when deprived of them! "

An old manuscript, dated 1695, gives us the following curious custom: " In all these Islands they take a sort of fish about a foot in length, by angling upon the shore; this they call the " Whistling Fish " and giving it that name because they whistle whilst they take it, this fish rarely taking the bait unlesse they doe, for whereas if the anglers whistle and make a vocall noise (which they usually do alternately) they bite very freely; For which reason whistling, etc., is constantly used in the catching of this fish, which is taken here in great plenty. I confess I was at first dubious of this relation, till my informer attested to the truth of it with some asseveration and since I have had it confirmed to me by severall other credible persons, so that I am satisfyed—whistling is us'd, but the fish be sensible of that noise or it be only an imagination of the fisherman that they are soe, I cannot disowne but that I am still in doubt." A further paragraph adds that: "The Islands export nothing but fish, but this they do in great quantityes, practically, Codds, Lings, Pollocks, Mackerells, Schads, Soales, Plaish, Turbets, Congers—Mullets and Wraths, yearly to Italy, France and Spain."

The manuscript continues: "In the Islands of St. Martin and St. Mary they have a sort of bituminous earth in great plenty. They use it for fire and indeed burnes very well only it emits a sulphurous smell. 'Tis the only fewell they have, there being no coal nor any trees, not soe much as a shrubb, except brambles, furzes, broom and holly; and these never grow above four foot high . . . notwithstanding in the Island of St. Mary's, and in that of Tresco in digging the aforesaid bituminous earth they ordinarily find trees lodged among it . . . takes them to be oak and elm, and hath seen them from two foot six inches circumference, which is very large, and proportionable in length . . . part of the roots near the stem are not gone, as are also there main branches . . . nor any signs of ax or fire upon any of them and therefore cannot think that these Bog trees were either hewn or burnt up . . . seen them lying in the earth five or six feet deep.

"There is a sorte of oyly scumm swimming upon the water that arises from the Moores: in the trenches, and in the mudd of the Moores, they find eels very plentifully, and those many of them very large.

" . . . shipwrecks are very frequent. These the inhabitants call God's Blessings, they have a third part of all the goods they can save allowed by the proprietors of the ship, unless they hire ye assistance of the Islanders at such a determinate price to save all they can. In case all the men on board be cast away then all they can save is their owne."

Of the customs of the mid-eighteenth century, Heath reminds us of the proverb "Always a feast or a famine in Scilly," and that they had a very plentiful feast after harvest time called Nicla Thies. To illustrate the sentiment of detachment that these islands possessed, we quote Heath on the payment of workmen engaged on the King's works; he says: " part of the workmen were foreigners from England. No Islander is a freeholder, no person has a vote for choosing members of Parliament, nor are the islands represented by any, which shew that they are no part of the Country or County jurisdiction of Cornwall, but are distinct from both under a separate government! Here is no prison for the confinement of offenders, which shews that the people live upright enough not to require any, or that the place is a confinement of itself."

His comment on the drinking habits of the islands is " most of the private are public houses," and he complains frequently of the poor quality of the locally brewed beer, which, in his time, was 2d. a quart.

Of burials, Heath says that " when an islander dies, some friends set up the night with the dead, where it is a custom with them to feast cheerfully during the time . . . after the burial they express great concern for the loss of their friend, whom they lament is no more to be seen. The Chaplain performs the service and is well paid for his performance and claims, by the right of his office, a Scarf."

Of matrimony, he records that fifty years before his time banns were called and the chaplain paid five shillings, or not above half a guinea—or he would take what he could get. " Soldiers and persons, at that time, not in circumstances to pay for being joined, either joined themselves, or were joined gratis, *i.e.*, they were joined by vows, or taking one another's word, which was binding as long as they could agree. And this sort of conscientious binding was observed to hold as fast, and be as good a security of their future felicity, as if the parties had been tied together with the sacred shreds of matrimony."

Woodley, in 1822, seems to have nurtured a few grievances against the islanders; he complains of the difficulty of obtaining labour, particularly domestic, "because the women preferred kelping or knitting," and he comments unfavourably on the finery (straw hats and flying ribands) displayed on Sundays, which he thinks "ludicrous" by contrast with the week-day lack of shoes or stockings. He also speaks of the exorbitant charges "for any little service," but subsequent writers refute this statement and suggest that the islanders had a special price for the Rev. G. Woodley. One observation he makes is revealing: "there is an affected degree of independence amongst the Islanders, which even the pressure of poverty and affliction is unable to subdue"; this independence he refers to as "this sort of Spanish feeling"!

The military and ecclesiastical history of the islands up to the eighteenth century gives us very little information regarding the inhabitants, who were ruled by the Abbot and military Governors and by the stewards of the absentee landlords. From the time of Elizabeth to the refusal of the Duke of Leeds to renew his lease in 1834, tenure was short so that there was little security or encouragement to accumulate family fortunes in buildings or farmland.

The population, excluding the military, has been computed, from various sources, as follows:—

A.D.	
1700	1,000
1750	1,400
1814	2,358
1939	1,780
1949	1,450

composed as follows:—

St. Mary's	1,025
Tresco	191
St. Martin's	110
Bryher	65
St. Agnes'	59

A market was instituted at Hugh Town in 1823. In 1747, The Lord Proprietor provided for the education of twelve poor children gratis; they were:—

Joseph Randall
Ann Chown
William Michel
Walter Banfull
Hugh Watts
Thomas Nichols
Isabella Henderson

and the son of the following :

John Davies
Henry Wood
Peter Symons
Edward May
Sarah Watts
William Trenear

A "baker's dozen" whom the clergyman, Mr. Lanyon, agreed to teach for a salary of twelve shillings per annum!

After the Dissolution, the ecclesiastical administration of the Islands was somewhat anomalous, and it was not until 1836 that the Islands were declared by Act of Parliament to be within the jurisdiction of the Bishop of Exeter. In the year 1660 the church at Old Town, St. Mary's, was constructed on the site of an older Norman structure, and when this fell into decay the new church at Hugh Town was constructed, and completed in 1838.

In Tresco there was a small church whose origin is shrouded in uncertainty, but which existed in 1798; it was enlarged in 1824 and 1835, and finally replaced by the present church in 1879. Bryher had its church in 1742, which was enlarged in 1928; St. Martin's church was enlarged in 1790 and restored early in the nineteenth century. St. Agnes' church was erected sometime in the sixteenth or seventeenth century and destroyed in a gale. In the eighteenth century a second church was constructed by the inhabitants from the proceeds of a wreck or the salvage of a vessel; this also was destroyed and the present church erected early in the nineteenth century.

There has been an Anglican clergyman resident on St. Mary's since 1662, who, however, in Heath's time (1750) had neither institution, induction nor visitation from the Bishop, holding his appointment from the Lord Proprietor and receiving the keys from his Agent. The "Off" Islands have had curates only since 1842, previous to which date the "Off" Islands were served mainly by laymen. The Society for Promoting Christian Knowledge founded "The Scilly Mission" in 1765, and continued to supply Missionaries to the "Off" Islands until 1842 both for religious instruction and secular education. Schools were built on St. Martin's and St. Agnes in 1830.

A Roman Catholic Church was built near the present harbour in 1240 and dedicated to St. Martin.

The Baptist Society came to Scilly in 1814 and flourished until the late 'forties, when its activities ceased owing to an unfortunate controversy amongst the members.

The Bible Christian Society established itself in 1821, and in the following year numbered 144 adherents; chapels were constructed in St. Mary's, St. Martin's (1823) and St. Agnes (1832). In 1827 Mr. William O'Bryan visited Scilly and the members of the Society afterwards became known as Bryanites. The United Methodist

Society, the United Free Church and the Methodist New Connexion amalgamated in 1907 to form the United Methodist Society, and the final reunion, Wesleyan Methodist Church, the Primitive Methodist Church and the United Methodist Church was formally sealed in 1932.

Woodley (1822) speaking of religion in his time, says that the Scillonians' behaviour at Church was decent and exemplary; they pay such attention to the external duties of religion that in St. Mary's and Tresco, where dissenters have established themselves, many of the people, halting between two opinions, " repair to the meeting-house in the morning, to Church in the forenoons and afternoons, and again to the Meeting in the evening."

Sundays were so very crowded with services of one kind and another that the Sunday School had, at one time, to be held on Saturday afternoons!

John Wesley visited the Isles in 1743 in a boat borrowed from the Mayor of St. Ives, but the Society was not established until 1788, and in 1792 the membership reached 150; the original Chapel was erected in 1790 and the existing one completed in 1828.

Of royalties who have visited the Islands, the earliest record is of King Athelstan, in A.D. 936, followed by King Olaf Trygvasson; Svein Ashlifahson, " King of Orkney and Caithness"; Charles I, when Prince of Wales; his son, Prince Charles (afterwards Charles II); Queen Victoria, with Prince Albert and the Prince of Wales, in 1847; King Edward VII in 1902; King George V (when a midshipman); Edward, Prince of Wales, in 1921, and again in 1933.

Queen Victoria's visit was unexpected, but she was received with due ceremony and drove through the Town and up to Star Castle. On the return journey the coachman mistook the way and commenced to descend the steep declivity from the Garrison Gateway to the Town;

one of the horses stumbled and alarmed the Royal party —it is said that the Queen's nerves had been shaken by an attempt on her life a short time previously—and they alighted and completed the journey on foot.

The Prince of Wales (now the Duke of Windsor) came to Star Castle by seaplane from Falmouth in 1933 and inspected the tenants of the Duchy on the Garrison.

The Islands are now administered by a Council (Isles of Scilly Order, 1890), consisting of a Chairman, four Aldermen and twenty Councillors, twelve of whom are elected from St. Mary's, three from Tresco, two from St. Agnes', two from St. Martin's and one from Bryher. The Chairman is nominated by the Duchy of Cornwall.

The Council is the Rating, Highway, Sanitary, Licensing and Education Authority for the Islands and has certain powers of a County Council.

Five Justices of the Peace are appointed.

The heritage of the Island as an independent and self-administered unit goes back many years. Upon the completion of the work of the Select Vestry, Administrative Powers for the Council to carry out its functions in relation to Local Government Services were granted by means of Provisional Orders, from 1890 up to the date of the last Order, viz., 20th January, 1943. For Local Government purposes the Council of the Isles of Scilly is a County Council, Urban District, and Rural District Council. As a County Council its functions cover Education, Agriculture, Public Assistance, Mental Deficiency, Lunacy, Police, and in the early stages of the War, and during the War, it carried out its functions as a scheme-making authority for Air Raid Precautions. Its Urban and Rural Powers are covered by the Public Health Acts 1875-1936 as specifically mentioned in the Provisional Orders. Exchequer grants in aid of Education (and the late War A.R.P.) are receivable. After taking into account these grants the net cost of carrying out all Services in the Islands has to be met from the Rates.

The Islands are Parcel of the Possessions of the Duchy of Cornwall, and the interests of the inhabitants are carefully safeguarded by those responsible for the administration of the Duchy.

The R.M.S. Scillonian, which provides a regular Service between Penzance and St. Mary's, is owned by the Scillonians, and there is a daily Air Service, all the year round, between Land's End and St. Mary's.

THE SMITH DYNASTY: 1834-1922

For more than two years, from 1831 to 1834, the Islands were directly under the Crown, and during this period the building of the Church at Hugh Town was commenced and an extension of the pier to Rat Island was contemplated.

In 1834 a member of an old Hertfordshire family, Augustus John Smith, leased the Islands from the Crown for a period of three lives; the terms of this lease were altered in 1920 to enable the Duchy of Cornwall to carry out extensive improvements in the buildings and amenities of their property—it was said that some £70,000 was expended. Under the new terms, Tresco, Samson and the uninhabited islands were retained by the present representative of the Smith family, and the other islands came directly under the administration of the Duchy. Tresco is leased for 99 years from 1929 and the uninhabited islands are leased for 31 years from the same date.

Augustus Smith's rule was well suited to the needs of a community that had for years been struggling against economic difficulties without achieving any cohesion or settled plan, suffering from absentee proprietorship and a system of land tenure as unsatisfactory as could have been devised.* He completed, according to the terms of his lease, the new church building and the extension of the pier at Hugh Town; he built a house at Tresco, now called "The Abbey," alongside the ruins of St. Nicholas Abbey, and laid out the magnificent sub-tropical gardens which have become world-famous.

*The law of majorats, or primogeniture, was not operative in the Islands; on the death of a tenant his land was divided up amongst all his children and, in consequence, the farms eventually became sub-divided into minute and scattered patches.

By virtue of land tenure Augustus Smith ruled the Scillies as Lord Proprietor for 39 years; his tasks, to put some semblance of order in the lives of the inhabitants and to find a solution to the apparently insoluble economic problems, were crowned with success.

Augustus Smith's first task was to put right an accumulation of abuses that had grown up following the rule (or misrule) of a succession of agents of the Godolphin-Osborne family; the situation demanded drastic action and a disturbance of the assumed vested rights and traditions of the inhabitants. His first concern was to re-allot the farm lands so that each farmer had a sufficient and compact portion of suitable land to which the eldest son should succeed. The other children had to find other employment. There was, however, plenty of work for those who were unfortunate in this rearrangement of the tenancies and for all able-bodied men, for not only was the new addition to the pier and the work on the new Church at Hugh Town completed, but new roads were constructed throughout the Islands and the Lord Proprietor's residence commenced. Later, new schools were built on all the main islands and the attendance ensured by a levy of 3d. per week on all families who were in a position to send their children but who might neglect to do so; in effect, compulsory education was established in the Scillies thirty years before it became Law on the Mainland.

The result of this universal education may be appreciated, after three generations, in the present-day Scillonians, who are all well-read and intelligent and whose mental horizon bears no relation to their physical horizon; their speech is almost pure English and has little, if any, trace of provincial dialect or idiom. Another result is that Scillonians, when they leave the Islands, are capable of holding responsible positions, and all over the world Scillonians may be found, some of whom are administrators, judges, lawyers, doctors, etc., while many have attained success in commerce.

In the conditions consequent on the new régime, which directly provided the basis for sound economic effort, and the stimulus to persevere, the Scillonians financed, without any direct help from the Lord Proprietor, a great development of the local shipbuilding industry which had been initiated by them as early as 1825. By the middle of the nineteenth century there were no less than five shipbuilding yards at St. Mary's, and when the ships were built they were manned and skippered by Scillonians, and the ships and cargo were the property of shareholders, who were all Islanders. To many, the coming and going of shipping afforded the opportunity of emigration to the Colonies.

The Scillonian shipbuilding yards continued until about 1870, when wooden ships were being supplanted by iron. The largest was the "John Banfield," of 528 tons, and the growth of the industry may be judged from the following table:

Wooden ships registered in Scilly:

In 1825	there were	15	with a tonnage of	574 tons.
In 1838	,, ,,	50	,, ,,	3,062 tons.
In 1851	,, ,,	59	,, ,,	6,843 tons.
In 1864	,, ,,	35	,, ,,	6,148 tons.

The Scillonian Captains traded all over the world, though the majority, probably, were engaged in conveying potatoes and other freights from ports in Ireland to the Mediterranean. St. Mary's, in the height of the shipping boom, was said to have been the richest place for its size in the Kingdom!

Augustus Smith introduced new and better varieties of early potatoes to the Islanders; he did not, however, confine his activities to the Islands; he was Liberal Member of Parliament for Truro from 1857-1865, and held many honorary positions in the County. He died in 1872 and was succeeded by his nephew, Lieut. T. Algernon Smith-Dorrien, who then assumed by letters patent the additional name of Smith under the provisions of the Will, and carried on the work initiated by his uncle for the welfare of the Islands.

The famous Tresco Gardens, laid out by Augustus Smith on the site at one time prepared by the Benedictine monks, were improved by his successors, rare plants were obtained from all over the world, and the old Scillonian sea-captains in their voyages in the tropics brought back strange roots. The gardens are ideally sited and sheltered, and many tropical and sub-tropical plants flourish in the open; indeed, it is claimed that several botanical specimens have never been successfully cultivated elsewhere north of the Mediterranean.

These gardens have always been most generously open to the public.

The present representative of the family, Major A. A. Dorrien-Smith, D.S.O., D.L., J.P., who succeeded his father in 1918, resides at Tresco Abbey and is Chairman of the Isles of Scilly Council and Chief Magistrate for the Islands, so that, although he no longer leases all the islands, the Scillonians have the benefit of his wide knowledge of affairs and of his counsel and advice on all matters that concern them and, in particular, in horticultural subjects and in the cultivation and marketing of the early flowers.

ROBERT MAYBEE

Robert Maybee was a ballad singer and poet who ought to have existed in the Dark Ages, but who was born on St. Mary's in 1810 and died there in 1884. In his later years he was reduced to hawking fruit and doing odd jobs about the islands, but his songs have always been treasured by Scillonians; his native charm and simplicity of character shines through all the records he has left behind him, and the history of the Islands has been enriched by his artless but no doubt accurate descriptions of the life around him in the nineteenth century. He was an insignificant-looking little man with weak blue eyes and curly hair, and he could neither read nor write.

The following is one of Robert Maybee's word pictures describing the wreck of the "Association," the "Eagle" and the "Romney" in 1707, when Sir Cloudesley Shovel, so the story goes, refused to take the advice of one of his crew, a Scillonian, and ran his ship on the rocks with the loss of two thousand men.

"Dark on the Gilstons' rocky shore
  The mist came lowering down,
And night with all her deepening gloom
  Put on her sable crown.

From sea a wailing sound is heard,
  And the seamew's shrilly cry,
And booming surge and shrieking birds
  Proclaim strange danger nigh.

Wrong you steer, Sir Cloudesley, sure;
  The rocks of Scilly shun;
Northern move, or no sailor here
  Will see to-morrow's sun.

Hold, wretch! Dare tell your Admiral
What dangers to evade?
I'll hang you up on yon yard-arm
Before your prayers are said.

Oh, Admiral, before I die
Let someone read aloud
The one hundred and ninth dread Psalm
To all this sailor crowd.

Let it be done, cursed mutineer;
As if I know not how
To steer my Association clear
Of every danger now.

The Psalm was read, the wretch was hung;
Drear darkness stalked around;
Whilst all aloft the dead man swung,
Three ships had struck the ground.

How sad and awful was the sight,
How black and dark the shore.
Two thousand souls went down that night,
And ne'er saw daylight more.

One man alone of that brave crew
Was saved to tell the tale.
How swift and sure God's vengeance came;
He can alone prevail."

EXTRACTS FROM "SIXTY-EIGHT YEARS' EXPERIENCE ON THE SCILLY ISLANDS"

By Robert Maybee

"WHEN I was young I many times wished I had been a scholar, that I might have written a long history of the Scilly Islands; but, being no scholar and, in fact, unable to read or write, it was useless my thinking of making a book, so I gave up all idea of it until the year 1883. I was working in Tresco at that time, and in the evenings, when I had leisure, walking around the hills and thinking of what had passed on the Islands in my lifetime, I found that I could remember everything that had happened in the islands for 68 years just as if it had occurred on that day. It then came into my mind that I would have a little book written if I could get someone to write it for me as I told it to him, about changes in life and trade and ship-wrecks and loss of life and also some pieces of poetry of my own composition . . . .

" I asked the master of the house at which I lodged whether he would write a little book for me in the winter evenings, and he was agreeable. The first line of this book was put to paper on 5th November, 1883, my age at that time being 74 years. I chose that day to begin my book because 50 or 60 years ago it used to be a great holiday on this island, being known as " Ringing Tide," when all the boys were looking forward to having a day's holiday to ring the church bell.

" At that time Scilly was a fine place for catching fish. There were more than four times as many men on St. Mary's as there are now, and they were bigger and a much stronger race of people than the present inhabitants. They did not call themselves fishermen because a living could not be made out of fishing in those days; fish would not sell, as every man on the island could get as much as he liked to go after. It made no difference what their employment was—after they left work those who had no boats to go in could go out on the rocks and catch as many fish as they could carry home every night through the summer. In those days there were five draw-seines on St. Mary's, one on Tresco and one on Bryher, where they used to get all their winter fish. In St. Agnes'

Cove the rule they had at that time was to shoot a buoy in the Cove with the name of the seine on it; they who shot the first buoy had the first turn, and so on all the season. St. Agnes' people had Monday nights given to them to haul, Tresco and Bryher followed in their turn with St. Mary's, and St. Martin's people hauled at Ganelle Bar. After they had as much fish as they wanted any other people were at liberty to go there. This fishing began in the latter part of August and finished about the end of October, and during that time everyone on the islands would get as much fish as they wanted. I have been there myself at different times, and had to leave a large quantity of fish on the beach which the boats would not bring away. The 4th, 5th and 6th November were the days on which they settled for the fishing season, and they made a great holiday of the occasion. Fifty years ago there were 23 public houses on St. Mary's and companies in all of them every evening; at this time there are only five and you will scarce see a man belonging to the island in any one of them—that is one great change that has taken place.

"I was born on 1st April, 1810, on the Head of the Peninnis, at St. Mary's, one of the Scilly Islands in the County of Cornwall, and that was my home till I was 42 years of age. My father was a native of the Isle of Wight, in the County of Hampshire, and came to the Scilly Islands to work the windmill that now stands on the Head of Peninnis. After the machinery was all taken out of the mill, it was fitted out for a signal station and now goes by the name of Rowel's Tower. My father had a house built about 60 yards to the east of the tower, and there he resided till the year 1834, when he died. Peninnis at that time was considered one of the pleasantest places on the island by visitors; it was a large open downs with no hedge on the west side of it till you got half-way to Buzza's

Hill, and it was covered with long heath and wild flowers of various kinds which made it very pleasant in the summer time. It was about three-quarters of a mile from Hugh Town, with a footpath to it from Port Cressa close by the seashore.

"The weather was different in those days to what it is now. The summers were very hot and we sometime had calm weather for three or four weeks at a time, with a great number of small fishing boats all along the coast fishing, which made it very pleasant for travellers: and in winter-time, with an easterly wind, there was a great number of ships coming in through the Sound every day, and a great many people used to go out to see them come round Peninnis Head. On the east side of Peninnis was Old Town Bay: a large pilot boat, two six-oared gigs and eight smaller boats belonging to Old Town were kept there, which could be manned at any time at a quarter-hour's notice, so that there was something new every day. I can remember everything that has happened on the islands since I was 5 years of age. The great battle of Waterloo was fought on the 18th June, 1815, and shortly after that, peace was proclaimed and a public dinner was held at St. Mary's in the open air and the town lit up well that night. I can remember being there with my father and mother: there were big guns mounted all round the Garrison which used to be fired on certain days in the year, such as the Queen's birthday. There were 100 soldiers in the Garrison, who used to march to church every Sunday and play the drum and fife as they marched: and a large number of men-of-war were coming and going every day. The captains and officers and their boat crews would be ashore walking up and down the streets, so you see there was more life in Scilly 68 years ago than there is now.

"After the French war was over, the 20 or 30 invalids who had been doing garrison duty were pensioned off with a small sum of money and they all stopped on the island till they died. Peninnis at that time was one of the best places for catching fish from the rocks. The pensioners, not having much work to do, often came out to catch fish mornings and evenings—some for pleasure and some for pastime: and after that most of the ladies and gentlemen in the town used to come out for pleasure. I have known as many as 40 or 50 people to be on the different rocks fishing on a fine summer's evening, and that was carried on for many years. In those days people could catch as much fish as they wished to have by going to the rocks to get them. When I was about 8 or 9 years old I could go down to the rocks at any time of the day and catch more small whiting fish than two men can get at this time by sailing all round the islands in a boat—unless it is at a time when the fish are in. There are 11 rocks around Peninnis where we used to go to fishing. I shall name them. Beginning at the west side of Peninnis, there is Carn Michael, The Chair, The Murre, Deep Water, High Jolly, Low Jolly, Louise's Rock, Humphrey's Rock, New Jolly, Westward Carn and East Carn Lee. I was so much used to these rocks that I could come up over them in the darkest hour of the night, and many times, after all my company have gone, I have stayed behind myself to catch a conger. Sometimes I should get one or two and get them up over the rocks at 12 o'clock at night. I should not like to be there at this time to get up empty-handed, for I do not think I should get up at all!

"Fifty years ago in Old Town there were between 40 and 50 strong, able men, and they most of them got their living by labouring and fishing, piloting and making kilp. At that time, by making kilp in the summer season, men could get very good wages when it was a dry summer.

The first kilp I can remember was £5 a ton, and almost every person on the island was working on it that summer. There are but three or four people on the island who can remember anything about kilp-making, so I will give you an account of how it is done. They would begin to make kilp in March month all around the island as soon as they could get any of the drift-weed in. They most commonly used to go two families together: there were but three or four horses and carts on the island at that time and the seaweed used to be brought up in baskets by men, women and children, and every party had its own piece of ground to dry it on. The weed was spread and, if the weather was dry in a day or two it was turned over and when it was properly dry it was all made up in cocks, just like hay, above high-water mark where the sea could not come to it, and then the weed would be saved. After it had been in cocks for some time, and the weather being fine for burning it, they would have pits dug in the sand in the shape of a pan, quite small at the bottom and paved with small stones, and afterwards built around with single stones to a height of about two or three feet. The women would burn most of the kilp and the children would bring the weed to them while they were doing it, so that the men could do other work between times. All through the kilping season they would light up the kilp between eight or nine o'clock in the evening, putting on the weed in handfuls as fast as it would consume. After the kilp was burnt, six or eight men would come with kilp rakes to strike the kiln—that is, to work the kilp up—and when it was worked up it was like so much hot lead. They might have to work up as many as eight kilns, so they would have to run from one to another till they had completed all of them. There might be 40 or 50 kilns burning around St. Mary's in one day, so that each party would have to do its own work. The next morning a man would go down with a bar and raise the kilp up out of the pit; it would come out in a hard lump of about three hundredweight: it was then broken up in handy lumps and put under the cliff, and the pit was cleared out for burning again the next day; and so they would continue their work till August month, getting as much seaweed as they possibly could. Everyone knew his own ground for drying the seaweed just the same as going in his fields to work.

"In the summer days kilp was being made on the six islands, and some days there would be as many as 100 kilns burning on the different islands. The smoke would come from the kilns as thick as it would from a steamer when new coals were put in: on a calm day the smoke would go straight up (a light smoke, almost white) and that would look grand in this day.

"There were five kilp-merchants on the island; they were all shopkeepers, selling groceries and drapery, so that all the people who worked about the kilp would go and take up anything they wanted. This work was finished in the middle of August and the kilp was then all shipped off to Bristol to make glass and soap. This work was carried on till the year 1835, when the last kilp was burned on the islands. Few persons made kilp that year and it was sold for 30s. per ton.

"The harvest now begins. There were fine crops of grain on the island at that time and every man and woman that could reap was employed to save the harvest: the grain was all cut with a reap-hook and the farmers were very particular as to how it was cut, especially the barley, which was spread thin on the ground so as to cover it all over in order to get it well dried. It was all used for making bread: they would leave it on the ground for six or seven days and then bind it and make it up in round mows in the fields and leave it for three or four weeks before bringing it into the mowhay. The main thing farmers looked for in those days was to get a good harvest and save their 12 months bread in good condition. The grain would all be got into the mowhays by the latter part of September and then they would begin to get up the late crop of potatoes. Every man and boy would be employed, just as they are in this day, getting out the early crop: men's wages were 1/6 a day and find themselves, or 1/3 a day and have meat at the house of the farm they were working on. They had their choice as to which they would take; men with families would take 1/6 a day and go to their own homes, as living was very cheap at that time. It was only 3d. a day for three good meals to the young men who used to have their meat where they worked, and I think they got the best of it at the end of the week.

" The potatoes were of much better quality than those grown at present and were sold for 2/- per bushel all the year round. Every labouring man who had no potatoes of his own would take in his winter's stock when he was digging—30 or 40 bushels, according to the number of his family—so that they should not fall short until the next crop. This was the way the work was carried on in St. Mary's until the disease got into the potatoes.

" Every family on the island used to have as much fish as they could make use of in the 12 months without any cost, except the salt to save them. Every man could go and catch his own fish after finishing his day's work, whatever his employment may have been.

" Every householder on the island, whether a farmer or not, kept some pigs, and had a piece of ground by the house for growing potatoes to feed them. They would all have a pig to kill about Christmas-time, weighing from 16 to 18 score—pigs at that time being very large in the island; particularly about Old Town they would have them from 24 to 30 score weight, and their pork was better

the present day. Pork was sold then for 3d. per pound by the side. and sometimes less; and best cuts of beef were sold on the market for 5d. per pound and other parts for less. The cattle were small, the average weight of a bullock being from 4 to 4½ cwt. The winter bullocks were all fed on potatoes with a little dry meal, and the beef was richer and had a better flavour than we get now. Veal sold for 3d., mutton for 3d. to 4d. per lb.; young fowls for 1/- a pair; eggs 3d. to 4d. a dozen; and fresh butter 8d. lb.
and sweeter than that of any of the small pigs killed in

"With the first strong breeze of wind we got from the east after the harvest, a great number of ships would come into the harbour. Vessels in those days were of a different class to those in use at present, they were not built to beat to the wind but to sail before it, so that all the vessels that got into the Bristol Channel had to wait till the wind turned to the eastward before they could sail. When it came to a strong south-east wind they would all set sail, bound for the South Channel; when they came to the Land's End they would all bear away for Scilly and come in a fleet. I have known as many as 200 come in one day, reaching from Giant's Castle up to the Roadstead, three and four abreast, which was a grand sight; and after that vessels would be coming in every day, while the wind was to the eastwards.

"The Roadstead, New Grimsby Harbour, Old Grimsby Harbour and St. Ellen's Pool would be as full of vessels as they could hold; and these ships must have left a great deal of money in the islands, as they had to lie there till the wind shifted to the westward. If it changed on a fine day, all those vessels left the harbour on that day: that is a sight we cannot see nowadays, which is another great change that has taken place in 68 years.

"When we got east wind further on in the winter it was very cold. The weather was very different 50 years ago to what it is now. We used to get a great deal of calm weather, with the sun very hot, and the hotter the summer, the colder was the winter; I have known everything frozen up for three or four weeks at a time. In cold winters there used to be a large number of wild fowls on the islands: I have run around Peninnis on a cold morning to keep myself warm and have put up as many as 20 cocks before breakfast. In some cases they may have dropped and I may have put the same bird up again, but woodcocks were very plentiful on the islands at that time and, after heavy rain on the flat part of Peninnis where shallow pools of water would stand, I could put up hundreds of snipe every day. No person would fire at a snipe in those days, so they were never disturbed unless anyone was walking on the downs. A great quantity of wild geese and duck used to come to this spot in the winter. Many people were in the habit of walking around Peninnis to look at the vessels coming in, and some would take their guns with them and shoot a goose or duck, whichever they could fall in with. There were hundreds of lapwing and plover on the islands, and everyone was allowed to carry a gun who could buy one, but there were not many people here who cared much for shooting.

"The summer of 1824 was the finest and pleasantest I ever knew; in April, May and June we had fine warm pleasant weather, with some showers to keep the crops growing. The stems of the potatoes were three or four feet long that summer and, there being no wind to hurt the crops, they grew as high as five feet, and in many places higher than the hedges, so that when two or three adjoining fields were in potatoes they looked like one field. When in bloom the potatoes carried a pink blossom, so that the islands looked like a flower garden.

"In 1825 occurred the season that was called the famine season, when everything was dried and burnt up by the hot sun—after heavy rain for one and a half hours in the latter part of May not a drop of rain fell till September. This occurred at a time when kilp was being made on the islands and most of the people working at it; they had a chance of keeping themselves cool by wading about in the sea during the hot weather. In the middle of the day the sand was so hot that nobody could stand on it for a moment. Several wells were dried up and also all the pools where the cattle drank, except a little in the lower moors, to which they were all driven. We had to fetch our water from Piper's Hole, at the head of Peninnis. The sun was so hot that summer that when the small pits were filled with water by the high tides, the water would be dried up and the salt left during the neap tides. I have gone down many times and scraped up 10 or 12 pounds that had been made by the sun, and you could get salt every neap tide through that summer. The hardest gale of wind that ever blew on the islands occurred on 13th February, 1833, from the westward. It was almost impossible for a man to stand on his legs, and we could not look to windward. A heavy rowing gig belonging to Tresco was up on the bank, and the force of the wind took her up in the air and the weight with which she came down broke her in pieces.

"It was thought that after the kilping was done away with people would not get any employment, but about that time shipbuilding began to go ahead on the islands. Small schooners were built for the fruit trade to St. Michael's and other ports and it was found to pay so well that they could not get men to build them fast enough; they had to get shipwrights from wherever they could. There were four master builders and all the young men were learning the shipwright business, which increased very fast; and shortly after that they began to build larger vessels for the Mediterranean and different parts of the world, and this trade was carried on for a great number of years. The shipowners had got some very fine vessels — large schooners, brigs and barques—trading in most parts of the world.

" The fleet of ships belonging to the Scilly Islands numbered between 60 and 70; the greater part of them were owned by the inhabitants, and it was said that they were paying thirty per cent. at that time. A shipping company was got up in £10 shares and did very well, and after that another was started in £5 shares, so that every person who had any money to lay out might have a chance of getting good interest for it. I belonged to the last company that was got up, and I believe most of the people on the islands who could raise £5 or £10 belonged to it to try their luck. There was £5,100 laid out in vessels, and after they had been running two years the accounts were made up, and owing either to bad captains or mistakes, the shares that were bought at £5 were only worth £2. Most of the small shareholders sold their shares at £2 and the company was broken up; but some of the large shareholders kept one of the vessels and run her for a great number of years, almost bringing the shares up to £5 again.

" Since that time, as fast as shipping has got up it has gone down again. At one time there were nearly 70 ships belonging to Scilly, and now there is only one little coal vessel of 100 tons belonging to the port.

" It was about this time that they found out the market for early potatoes which brought high prices for a number of years. It was almost like coining money, and it was said that at that time the island was the richest place in the world for the number of people in it. It is not only the shipping that has failed, but every trade on the island. There is scarcely any work to do now. You will see many people standing about for want of work to do, who would willingly take any work they could get for low wages.

"The longest easterly wind I ever remember was in 1853; it commenced in February and lasted till the latter part of May, making between 13 and 14 weeks, with a great many strong breezes during the spring. There were nearly 100 sail of vessels lying in St. Mary's Roadstead in May and there was not a day they could get to sea.

"In 1854 we had a heavy storm of wind from the south-east; on the morning after the storm there was scarcely a green leaf to be seen on the island. Ten or 12 vessels were repaired on the island.

"In 1855 I engaged to work on the Trinity Works to build the lighthouse on the Bishop Rock. It was a very pleasant summer and I was much pleased with my employment. The labourers and bargemen were paid off on the last day of November, but the stone-cutters, carpenters and blacksmiths were all kept on three weeks later. The stones for the building were all worked in the yard on Rat Island. Shortly after I was paid off from this work I went to St. Agnes on a visit, and while on this island I met with a farmer who asked me if I would stay there and work for him all the winter. He had plenty of work for me to do till I wanted to ship on the Bishop Works again, and I should lose no time as when it was not fit to work out of doors he had plenty for me to do in the barn. He offered me good wages, victuals and lodgings. There was plenty of money being got in St. Agnes at that time. The farmer belonged to one of the pilot boats, and they were at sea every day in the winter when it was fit to go, and he was all behind with his work on the farm.

"I could not content myself on St. Agnes, but I was there all through the shortest days of the winter; they have five meals a day on this island . . . I worked on the Bishop Works five years, and on St. Agnes each winter of that time."

WRECKS, WRECKERS AND SMUGGLERS

THERE is an aprocryphal story of a Scillonian addition to the Litany: " We pray Thee, O Lord, not that wrecks should happen, but that if any wrecks should happen, Thou wilt guide them into the Scilly Isles for the benefit of the poor inhabitants." There is another yarn of an undignified scramble from church in the middle of a service, the minister leading the way, to the scene of a reported wreck. It was related of a clergyman of St. Agnes that, on being informed by the verger in the middle of his sermon of a wreck, he announced it from the pulpit: on the next occasion he said nothing, but walked to the church door and from there made his announcement, adding: " This time we all start fair ! "

There is not a tittle of evidence to justify the accusation against either Cornishmen or Scillonians of deliberate wrecking, and the stories of cows left to wander on the coast with lights attached to their tails, and similar absurdities, belong to the realm of fiction, but there is no doubt whatever that wrecks on Scilly were an intermittent, if not regular, source of income, and that in the course of time the islanders came to regard the proceeds of shipwrecks as part of their natural harvest. It is quite understandable that they should have been recorded as objecting to the erection of a lighthouse—" because it would rob them of ' God's Grace,' " *i.e.*, the produce of wrecks.

The Islands lie in the track of the main routes from America, the Mediterranean, Africa and the East, the British Isles, North Sea, Baltic, and Irish Sea and Bristol Channel, and there is probably more trans-ocean traffic around the Islands than at any other point on the globe. They have also the most formidable traps for the unwary mariner, variable currents and tides, and small, unpretentious but deadly rocks often wholly though insufficiently submerged. In the case of America they are the first landfall after a voyage of some 3,000 miles.

In the days of imperfect navigational instruments it is not surprising that very many wrecks occurred, but we believe that this chapter of Island history is now ended, thanks to " Radar," wireless, and all the modern technical improvements in the Science and Practice of Navigation.

Honour where honour is due, the Scillonians are, and have always beens *life-savers;* with no hope of reward and solely at the dictates of humanity, Scillonian boatmen have again and again risked, and often lost, their lives in order to save the crews of shipwrecked vessels. The records are full of heroic rescues against terrific odds and there is not one case, in the whole of history, of wrecking ! From the close of the seventeenth century to the present day, over 200 wrecks have occurred on the Scilly Isles alone, and all of these were fine, well-found ships, and most of them were abandoned and, in many cases, the crews perished.

The worst recorded disaster was that of Sir Cloudesley Shovel's fleet in 1707, when, on the return journey from Toulon, four ships struck on the Gilstone Rock, Scilly, and the flagship " The Association," the " Eagle " and the " Romney " were lost with all hands save only one man. About 2,000 men lost their lives. The only survivor, from the " Romney," saved himself by floating on a piece of timber to the rock Hellweathers, where he remained some days until he could be taken off. The body of Sir Cloudesley was washed ashore at Porthhellick, St. Mary's, where it was buried, later to be disinterred and placed in Westminster Abbey with great honour. Henry

Trelawney also lost his life in this wreck; he was the son of Bishop Trelawney, who was the hero of the Cornish song:—

"And shall Trelawney die?
Then twenty thousand Cornish men
Will know the reason why."

Amongst other naval vessels wrecked on the Scillies at different times were the sloop "Lizard" (1747), 100 men perished; the "Colossus" and a transport (1777); and the brigantine "Foster" (1833).

Of passenger steamers, the best known are the steam packet "Thames" (1841), in which 62 persons lost their lives; the "Delaware" (1871); the s.s. "Schiller" (1875), a mailboat from New York to Bremen, in which 311 persons lost their lives; and the s.s. "Minnehaha" (1910), which was afterwards refloated.

The stories of these wrecks produce some remarkable, almost miraculous, accounts of persons who have been saved in spite of the elements, but none so remarkable as that of the four men of the brig "Nerina" of which the following is a fully authenticated account*:—

"The brig 'Nerina,' of Dunkerque, sailed from that place on Saturday, the 31st of October, 1840, under the command of Captain Pierre Everaert, with a cargo of oil and canvas for Marseilles: her burthen was about 114 tons; the crew consisted of seven persons, including the captain and his nephew, a boy 14 years old.

"At three o'clock in the afternoon of Monday, the 16th of November, they were forced to heave-to in a gale of wind at about 10 or 12 leagues south-west of the Scilly Islands. At seven o'clock of the same evening, still lying-

*Quoted from L. C. Courtney's "Guide to Penzance"; from an account of the French Consular Agent, Penzance, 1840.

to under their close-reefed main-top-sail and balanced reefed main-sail, a heavy sea struck the vessel and she suddenly capsized, *turning completely bottom up*.

" The only man on the deck at the time was named Boumelard, who was instantly engulfed in the ocean. In the forecastle were three seamen—Vincent, Vantaure, and Jean Marie: the two former, by seizing hold of the windlass-bits, succeeded in getting up close to the keelson, and so kept their heads above water. Poor Jean Marie was not so fortunate; he must have been in some measure entangled, as, after convulsively grasping the heel of Vantaure for a few seconds, he let go his hold and was drowned. The other two, finding that the shock of the upset had started the bulkhead between the forecastle and the hold and that the cargo itself had fallen down on the deck, contrived to draw themselves on their faces close alongside the keelson (for it could not be reached on their hands and knees for want of height) towards the stern of the ship, from whence they thought they heard some voices.

" At the time of the accident the captain, the mate, Jean Gallo, and the boy, Nicholas Nissen, were in the cabin. The captain caught the boy in his arms, under the full impression that their last moments had arrived.

"The mate succeeded in wrenching open the trap-hatch in the cabin deck, and in clearing out some casks which were jammed in the lazarette (a sort of small triangular space between the cabin floor and the keelson, where stores are generally stowed away): having affected this, he scrambled up into the vacant space and took the boy from the hands of the captain, whom he assisted to follow them.

" In about half an hour they were joined by Vincent and Vantaure from the forecastle. There were then five individuals closely cooped together: as they sat they were obliged to bend their bodies for want of height above them, while the water reached as high as their waists; from which irksome position one at a time obtained some relief by stretching at full length on the barrels in the hold, squeezing himself up close to the keelson.

"They were able to distinguish between day and night by the light striking from above into the sea and being reflected up through the cabin skylight, and then into the lazarette through the trap-hatch in the cabin floor.

"The day and night of Tuesday, the 17th, and the day of Wednesday, the 18th, passed without food, without relief, and almost without hope; but still each encouraged the others, when neither could hold out hope to himself, endeavouring to assuage the pangs of hunger by chewing the bark stripped off from the hoops of the casks. Want of fresh air threatening them with death by suffocation, the mate worked almost incessantly for two days and one night in endeavouring, with his knife, to cut a hole through the hull. Happily the knife broke before he had succeeded in accomplishing his object, the result of which must have proved fatal, as the confined air alone preserved the vessel in a sufficiently buoyant state.

"In the dead of night of Wednesday, the 18th, the vessel suddenly struck heavily: on the third blow the stern dropped so much that all hands were forced to make the best of their way, one by one, farther towards the bows, in attempting which poor Vincent was caught by the water and drowned, falling down through the cabin floor and skylight.

"After the lapse of an hour or two, finding the water to ebb, Gallo got down into the cabin, and whilst seeking for the hatchet, which was usually kept there, was forced to rush again for shelter to the lazarette to avoid being drowned by the sea, which rose on him with fearful rapidity. Another hour or two of long suffering succeeded, when they were rejoiced to see by the dawning of the day of Thursday, the 19th, that the vessel was fast on rocks, one of which projected up through the skylight. The captain then went down into the cabin and found that the quarter of the ship was stoved and, looking through the opening, he called out to his companions above, 'Grace à Dieu, mes enfants, nous sommes sauvés! Je vois un homme à terre.' Immediately after this the man approached and put in his hand, which the captain seized, almost as much to the terror of the poor man as to the intense delight of the captain. Several people of the neighbourhood were soon assembled; the side of the ship was cut open and the poor fellows were liberated from a floating sepulchre after an entombment of three days and three nights in the mighty deep."

The spot where the vessel struck is called Porthellick, in the island of St. Mary's, Scilly: she must have been driven on the rocks soon after midnight at about the period of high water, and was discovered lying dry at about seven o'clock on Thursday morning by a man accidentally passing along the cliffs. In another half-hour the returning tide would have sealed their fate.

Not the least remarkable part of the narrative is that on the afternoon of Wednesday, the 18th, the wreck, floating bottom up, was fallen in with at about a league and a half distant from the Islands by two pilot boats, which took her in tow for about an hour, but their tow-ropes breaking and night approaching, with a heavy sea running and every appearance of bad weather, they abandoned her, not having the least suspicion that there were human beings alive in the hold of the vessel, which was floating with little more than her keel above water! Whilst, had the vessel not been so taken in tow, the set of the current would have drifted her clear off the Islands into the vast Atlantic!

St. Agnes' Lighthouse had the distinction of being the oldest but one of all the lighthouses in the British Isles, sometimes referred to as the Land of Lighthouses. The first was Winterton, in 1678; Scilly was the next, and Eddystone followed in 1694.

The Master Wardens and Assistants of the Guild or Brotherhood of the most Glorious and Undividable Trinity and of St. Clement, in the Parish Church of Deptford Strand, in the County of Kent, were granted by Letters Patent of King Charles II, dated 24th May, 1680 (32 Charles II), power and licence to erect and maintain one or more lighthouses upon any of the Islands and to receive such allowance for maintenance of the same "As should be thought fit and reasonable according to law."

During 1679 and 1680 the lighthouse on St. Agnes' Isle was accordingly built; a royal ship was told off to convey the Trinity Brethren thither and to await their pleasure. Captain Hugh Till and Captain Simon Bayly seem to have superintended the work.

The payment of the Light Dues, when it was kindled, was most strongly opposed, and stringent measures had to be taken with many ships in order to enforce payment. The net revenue derived by the Trinity House from the St. Agnes' light was £1,765 17s. 1d. in 1805, rising to £3,191 9s. 11d. in 1815.

The first light was probably made from glowing sea coal and was very defective, and not until 1807 was a satisfactory light installed. This consisted of 30 lamps burning spermaceti, and reflectors, 10 in each face of a triangular frame, with a circular motion.

The Bishop Lighthouse, which probably shares with the Eddystone the title of the best known lighthouse in the world, was first constructed of cast iron in 1850, but was completely wrecked before it had been put into use; a second structure of stone replaced it, and this again was strengthened and largely rebuilt in 1887. The height above sea level is 160 feet. Throughout it was built by members of the Douglass family, and William Tregarthen Douglass, M.Inst.C.E., who completed it, was the son of Sir James Douglass, F.R.S., engineer-in-chief of Trinity House, who married a Scillonian, daughter of Captain James Tregarthen. The Bishop took the place of St. Agnes' Lighthouse, which was discontinued.

Later, lighthouses were constructed on Round Island and St. Mary's, and a lightship stationed at the Seven Stones Rocks, so that on a clear night it is possible to see from the Islands not only the lightship, but the Longships, the Wolf, St. Mary's, Round Island, and the Bishop lights, with flashes from more distant lights on the coast of Cornwall. In addition, there is every modern device such as beam radio, so that Scilly advertises her unpleasant and dangerous features very much more effectively than ever she had advertised to the world her title as Swinburne's "Small sweet world of wave-encompassed wonder." Finally, and it should be mentioned because it refuses audibly to be ignored on St. Mary's, whether by day or night, there is a bell buoy.

Smuggling, by its very nature, is a secret enterprise, conducted under cover of night, and it is quite impossible to obtain any direct evidence. According to the findings of the Penzance deputation to enquire into the distress of the "Off" Islands, the distress was largely due to the "entire suppression of smuggling by the preventive boat system, by the loss of which contraband the Islanders lost *their chief means of support*"!

Jessie Mothersole, in a chapter of her book entitled "Former Industries" (!), says that smuggling was a very popular employment and that even the Clergy engaged in it. She instances a report, we know not on what foundation, that the Rev. John Troutbeck, who wrote the Survey of the Islands in 1794, had to leave the Islands "from fear of the consequences of having taken part in it."

Alexander and Herbert Gibson, in their book of the "Isles of Scilly," mention a character named Uncle Bill, of Old Grimsby, who, after long years in the "Trade," became converted and developed into a local preacher; and Aunt Jane, of St. Agnes, "whose house was a veritable treasure of a hiding-place for the contraband." They add that smuggling spirits from France had its period and vanished. The smugglers used to row across to France in open six-oared gigs (some of these are still to be seen on the Islands) and return with ankers of spirit—a truly dangerous and venturesome voyage.

On islands nothing is secret, and a serious and continuous course of smuggling would need support from the great mass of public opinion. The Gibson brothers reveal their own sentiments in the following passage from their book:—"We have met people who were not only shy but ashamed of its being known that they were related to these grand old-world adventurers; but it seems to us that to have a dashing smuggler amongst one's ancestors should be regarded more as an interesting link with a picturesque past than a fact to be concealed. We have always thought that it was the sporting instinct as much as anything in the way of gain that induced them to run such risks as they did."

THE FLOWER INDUSTRY

" . . . . daffodils,
That come before the swallow dares, and take
The winds of March with beauty; violets dim,
But sweeter than the lids of Juno's eyes,
Or Cytherea's breath, ..."

(*Shakespeare*: *" The Winter's Tale "*)

NATURE provides the Isles of Scilly with a feast of colour all the year round, but especially in May and June when one may walk knee-deep over the springy cushions of thrift with their masses of delicate pink blooms and be dazzled by the blood-red splashes of sorrel and the golden trefoil and gorse; and in the background, there is always the vivid blue and green sea that here rivals the Mediterranean and the West Indies in clarity and in the depth of its colour.

One of the commonest flowers on Scilly is the mesembryanthemum, whose brilliant magenta and orange flowers are to be found on all the cottage gardens and walls. As though nature had not done enough, the islanders have planted every field of cultivable land with hedges of Euonymus, Veronica, Escalonia or Spittasporium in diminutive squares so as to present a chequerboard appearance. In these minute well-sheltered fields they cultivate the one hundred million blooms that are exported annually to Covent Garden; the main varieties are the Polyanthus Narcissus (from December to May), and Iris, Ixias, Stocks and Arums. The equable climate, and the fact that frost is almost unknown, enables the

Scillonian flower farmers to produce cut-blooms, cultivated in the open, considerably in advance of all others except their rivals in the Southern Coasts of France; some of the flowers are on the market early in December.

The origin of many of these bulbs is wrapped in mystery; it is unlikely that they were indigenous, the Scilly White may have come from the South of France, the Paper White from Italy and Spain, and others from China, but the magnificent varieties now marketed are the result of the recent fixation of new types. It is thought that the earliest bulbs, the Scilly Whites, were brought by the Monks of St. Nicholas' Abbey and became naturalised on all the islands. There is a local legend that the first bulbs were given to the wife of a governor of Star Castle, in return for some favour received, by a Dutch Merchant Captain. The lady, thinking they were onions, boiled some and, not liking the taste, threw the remainder into the Castle moat, where they flourished!

The first Scillonian to pay any attention to these flowers which were growing wild on St. Mary's, especially around the Garrison and in the dry moat of Star Castle, was William Trevellick, who for some years collected them secretly for his gardens at Rocky Hill Farm. In or about the year 1881 an experimental consignment of cut flowers was despatched to Covent Garden in, so it is said, a hatbox, and, the resulting cheque being unexpectedly large, the Scillonians were not slow to appreciate the possibilities. Mr. Richard Mumford, of Holy Vale, Mr. Hugh Watts and Mr. W. M. Gluyas, of Old Town, joined Mr. Trevellick and became the first of the flower farmers.

The successful and permanent establishment of this industry was, however, largely due to Mr. T. A. Dorrien Smith, as will be seen from the following statement, dated 1893, for submission to his Royal Highness the Prince of

Wales on behalf of the Trustees of the late Mr. Augustus Smith:—

"Mr. Dorrien Smith .. . endeavoured to improve the cultivation of early potatoes by the introduction of new seeds and fresh sorts; but owing to Foreign competition, their cultivation has proved to be too hazardous and speculative for the Islanders to embark in to any considerable extent.

"He next determined to introduce the cultivation of bulbs, and with this in view he spent some time in Holland, studying the system of cultivation there, and then imported by degrees large quantities of them, selling them at cost price to his Tenants. This has now become a very popular and the most lucrative industry there, and in favoured and sheltered spots can be successfully carried on, and so long as the fashion of bulb flowers continues, this industry promises to be a source of considerable profit to the Islanders. But its introduction has cost Mr. Dorrien Smith £10,000, expended in the purchase of bulbs, the erection of bulb and flower houses, etc."

Mr. T. A. Dorrien Smith went to Holland in the spring of 1882 and some 190 kinds of bulbs were planted in Tresco Abbey Gardens in the autumn of that year; he visited Messrs. Ware's grounds at Upper Tooting (then agricultural land) and also Messrs. Barr's nurseries, where many of the Incomparabilis, Barri and Ornatus hybrids were first raised—a few of these original kinds still exist in the Abbey gardens but they have long since been surpassed by better types of market flowers.

In 1885 the Isles of Scilly Bulb and Flower Association was formed. Annual Shows were held at St. Mary's and Mr. Dorrien Smith presented a silver challenge cup for the best exhibit of cut flowers.

Launch of the "David Auterson," St Mary's, 1871.

The Valhalla, Tresco. *Photo : King, Scilly.*

The fashion for cut flowers in English households was revived in or about the year 1873 and has been maintained ever since. Daffodils and Narcissi are the harbingers of spring and there can be no doubt that the Scillies help to sustain men and women in our great industrial cities during the " dog days " of winter.

The growth of the cut flower trade will be seen from the following table:—

1881	one box (realised £1)	
1885	65 tons of cut flowers	
1886	85	do.
1887	100	do.
1889	198	do.
1896	514	do.
1924	700	do.
1931	1,064	do.

and since then it has exceeded 1,200 tons!

There is no doubt that the flower trade came just in time to save the islands from destitution for it was introduced when the potato harvests—early potatoes had been a profitable crop since 1538—were failing and when shipping and ship building came to an end.

In later years, especially since the improved facilities for transport, the islanders have derived great benefit from an increasing number of visitors, who come, from March onwards, annually in ever increasing numbers but not, as yet, in sufficient crowds to spoil the peace and natural tranquillity of the Isles.

BIBLIOGRAPHY

1222	" Heimskringla " - - -	Snorri Sturluson
1478	" Itinerary " - - -	William of Worcester
1533	" Itinerary " - - -	John Leland
1602	" Survey of Cornwall " - -	Carew
1669	" Cosmo's Travels " - -	Duke of Tuscany
1676	" Memoirs " - - - -	Lady Fanshawe
1750	" Account of the Islands of Scilly "	Robert Heath
1756	" Observations " - - -	Dr. William Borlase
1794	" Survey " - - - -	Rev. John Troutbeck
1804	" History of Cornwall, with Supplement by Whitaker " -	Rev. R. Polwele
1810	" Report on the Scilly Islands " -	B. Tucker
—	" Climate of the Isles of Scilly " -	T. T. Macklin
—	" Cornwall as a Winter Resort " -	Kilts
1814	" Cornwall " - - -	Lyson
1822	" A View of the Present State of the Scilly Islands " - -	Rev. George Woodley
1849	" Sketches in the Scilly Isles " -	Lady Sophia Tower
1850	" A Week in the Isles of Scilly " (Revised by L. H. Courtney, 1867) - - - -	Rev. I. W. North
1852	" Scilly and its Legends " - -	Rev. H. J. Whitfeld
1855	" A Londoner's Walk to Land's End " - - - -	Walter White
1861	" Rambles in Western Cornwall "	J. C. Halliwell
1861	" Excursions in County of Cornwall, etc." - - -	" "
—	" The Cornish Excursionist " -	Anon
—	" Seaside Studies " - - -	G. H. Lewis
—	" Beautiful Islets of Britain " -	W. C. Dendy
—	" Guide to Mount's Bay, etc." -	By a Physician
—	" Lyonesse (revisited) " - -	Tonkin and Row

—	" The Cassiterides " - -	George Smith
—	" Rambles Beyond Railways " -	Wilkie Collins
1865	" Memoirs of W. Forster " -	
—	" Yachting Round the West of England " - - -	L'Estrange
1875	" Guide to the Scilly Isles " -	J. C. and R. W. Tonkin
1876	" A Botanical Trip to Scilly Isles "	W. Curnow
1884	" Sixty-eight Years' Experience on the Scilly Islands " - -	Robert Maybee
1885	" Dagonet on our Islands " -	G. R. Sims
1899	" Book of the West " - -	Rev. S. Baring-Gould
—	" The Wolf Rock Lighthouse " -	J. N. Douglas
1906	" Cassiterides and Ictis " - -	Thurstan Peter
—	" Guide to Penzance and Scilly " -	Anon
—	" Scilly and the Scillonians " -	J. G. Uren
—	" Faire Lyonesse " - - -	J. G. Owen
1910	" The Isles of Scilly " - -	Jessie Mothersole
1925	" The Scillonian Quarterly Magazine " - - - -	(First Number)
1932	" Cornwall and Scilly " (The County Archæologies) - -	H. O'Neill Hencken
1932	" King's Popular Guide " - -	C. J. King
—	" St. Michael's Mount " - -	Rev. T. Taylor
—	" The Isles of Scilly " - -	Alexander and Herbert Gibson
1934	" Isles of the Island " - -	S. P. B. Mais
1938	" Isles of Scilly Guide " - -	E. L. Bowley
1949	" Isles of Scilly Guide " - -	E. L. Bowley

POETRY

—	" Songs of the West " - -	Rev. S. Baring-Gould
1866	" Roathmere and other Poems " -	Sarah Eliza Tonkin
—	" The Ballad of the Royal Anne "	Crosbie Garstin

FICTION

— " Cornubia " - - - G. Woodley

— " Armorel of Lyonesse " - - Sir Walter Besant

— " Major Vigoureux " - - " Q " (Sir Arthur Quiller-Couch)

— " The Dominant Law " - - D. Lewis

— " Fairy Gold " - - - Compton Mackenzie

— " Miranda of the Balcony " - A. E. W. Mason

— " A Man of Moods " - - H. D. Lowry

— " Bazin's Gold " - - - E. Cornish

— " Wrecked on Scilly " - - M. Onley

— " Lost Land of King Arthur " - J. C. Waters

— " The Wreckers on the Longships " F. J. Cobb

INDEX

(Wherever possible, the narrative is arranged in chronological order.)

PAGE

A

Adams, Robert ... 81, 82, 83
Aeolian Cyme 5
Africa 21, 23
Albion 24, 25
America 13
Andalusia 26
Antoninus 107
Aristotle 30
Armada 6, 76, 79
Armorica 35, 110
Arras 24
Arrotrebae 18
Arthur, King 20, 46, 51, 53 60
Arundel 99
Arvad 22
Ascue 92, 93, 96
Ashford 114
Ashlifarson 65, 134
Ashurites 22
Athelstan ... 7, 48, 115, 134
Athenians 10
Atlantis 10, 13
Avalon 10
Avienus 24, 107

B

Banfields 112, 114
Baptists 133
Barentin 50, 69
Barrow 44
Bashan 22
Basset 89
Bastwick 98
Bedford Regiment 112
Bennett 100
Bergion 24
Bible Christian 113
Biddle 98
Bircherod 13
Blake 7, 92, 93, 95, 97
Blankminster 50, 70, 72, 73
Bluets 114
Bluett, Capt. 89
Borlase ... 15, 17, 31, 109, 116
Bowden 94
Briareus 15
Bristol 23
Brittany 7
Britons 7, 14
Bronze Age 16
Burghley 79, 82
Burn, Sir Clive ... 4, 8

C

Caesar, Julius 27
Camden 41, 111
Cape of Good Hope ... 23
Caractacus 107
Carew 83, 107
Carey 80
Celestin 68
Celtiberia 18
China 20, 28, 29
Chittim 22
Clarke 95
Coates 97
Coleshill 73
Colpepper 88
Conrad 7
Corbilo 33
Cosmo 99, 113
Courtney 158
Crassius 34, 35, 41
Crispe 89
Cromwell 98
Cronus 15
Crudges 112

PAGE

D

Damnonii 31, 110
Danes 7
Danvers 74
Declaration of War ... 6, 93
Demetrius 14
Dickenson 54
Diodorus 13, 23, 32, 34, 35
Dionysius 27
Domesday Book 105
Douglass 163
Druids 17, 18, 21, 31, 106, 109
Dunstonville 48, 67
Dutch 6

E

Edwards 112, 114
Egypt 16, 17, 22
Elishah 22
Ellis 114
Elysian Fields 10
Eustathius 111
Eva, Chas. A. 26
Ezekiel 22, 27

F

Fairfax 88, 91
Flecker, James Elroy ... 10

G

Gades ... 19, 21, 23, 27, 28
Gama, Vasquez da ... 23
Gandewan 71
Gauls 7, 18, 20, 21
Gebal 22
Genesis 27
Geryon 19
Gibraltar ... 10, 18, 29, 105
Gibson 40, 114, 164
Gilbert 110
Glasinnis 10
Gluyas 166

PAGE

Godolpin 76, 80, 81, 82, 83, 84, 86, 87, 97, 98, 100, 101, 112, 138
Gould, Baring 51
Grail, Holy 54
Grandison 68
Greeks 20, 22, 27
Grenadier Guards 112
Grenville ... 91, 92, 94, 96, 97, 99, 100

H

Hades 19
Hamely 73
Hamilco 24
Hamilton 98
Hanno 24
Heath ... 26, 37, 117, 119, 120, 122, 124, 126, 127, 130, 133
Heimskringla 62
Hencken, H. O'Neill 8, 13, 14, 25, 108
Hercules 19, 23, 24, 53, 119
Hermes 26
Herodotus 23, 29, 30
Hicks 114
Himkiss 100
Holy Island 25
Hooper, J. E. 8, 79
Howard 79, 81
Hull 68
Hunkin 98
Hurling ... ... 120—122

I

Iberians 7, 27, 34, 109
Iceland 6
Ictis 32
India 28, 29, 36
Ireland 7, 15, 25, 105
Ireton 98
Isle of Wight 32
Isles of the Blessed ... 7, 10

PAGE

J

Jane (Aunt) 164
Jenkins 114, 127
Jenner 110
Jerusalem 23

K

Kirk, H. W. 8
Kronos 15

L

Lanje, E. J. 8, 94
Lanyon 132
Laud 98
Layamon 54
Layard 16
Lebanon 22
Legge 114
Leland 49, 73
Leveck 94
Longfellow 65

M

Magnusson 62
Mais 7
Majendie 36
Malory 51, 53, 107
Marcus 41
Marseilles 27, 34
Maximus 41
McFarland 8, 112
Medina Sidonia 79
Mediterranean ... 7, 20, 21, 23
Melkarth 24
Menandez 79
Mictis 31
Midacritus 24
Milton 52
Monmouth, Geoffrey de ... 53
Moors 7
Morier (Morrers) 71
Morris, William ... 52, 62

PAGE

Mothersole, Jesse 124, 125, 164
Mount St. Michael 20, 31, 32, 35, 36, 46
Mumford 112, 114, 166

N

Nance 96
Narbona 34
Nelson 118
Nicholas, Saint 62
Nicla, Thies 124, 130
North 114

O

O'Bryan 133
Ochiltree 110
Oeconomicus 22
Oestrymnon 24

P

Pender 114
Pillars of Hercules 6, 10, 24, 29
Plato 13
Pliny ... 13, 18, 28, 31, 38
Plutarch 14, 15, 30, 46
Poer, William de ... 50, 72
Portugal 34
Posidonius 27
Primitive Methodists ... 134
Procopius 15
Ptolemy 33
Puffins 72, 80
Pyramids 16

Q

Quiller-Couch 101

R

Raleigh 79
Ringing Tide 125
Rogers, John 87
Roman Catholic 133
Romans 7, 22, 27, 28, 32, 40, 41, 107

PAGE

S

Sarah (Aunt) 126, 127
Sardus 111
Scott 52
Scylax 24
Senir 22
Seymour, Admiral Lord 8, 75, 76, 80
Shipbuilding 7, 139, 152, 153, 154
Shovel, Sir Cloudesley 141, 157
Sidon 20, 21, 27
Sidonia 79
Smith (Augustus) 114, 115, 137, 138, 139, 140 167
Smith (Dorrien) A. A. ... 140
Smith (Dorrien) T. A. 140, 166, 167
Smith (George) 30
Smyth 101
Solinus 31, 111
Spain ... 18, 21, 24, 26, 35
Spencer 52
Stanier, T. M. 8
Star Chamber 98
Strabo 5, 23, 27, 30, 34, 41, 46, 110
Sturluson 62
Sweden 6
Swinburne 52
Syria 17, 21, 25

T

Tacitus 30
Tarshish 22, 27, 29
Tartessus 19, 24, 29
Tavistock 66, 68, 69, 74, 75, 80
Taylor 34
Tennyson 51, 53, 60
Timaeus 18
Tregarthen ... 112, 114, 163

PAGE

Trelawney 158
Trevellick 166
Trevelyan 49
Trinity House 162
Trojan 20, 23
Tromp 6, 91, 93, 97
Tryggvasson 6, 62, 134
Troutbeck ... 109, 127, 164
Turks 7, 86, 87, 113
Tyre ... ... 19—23, 25—28

U

United Free Church ... 134
United Methodist 134

V

Vane 98
Veneti 35
Victoria 134
Vikings 7
Vyvyan 68

W

Walters, J. C. ... 32, 45
Waterloo 145
Watts 166
Wesley 134
Whitfield ... 55, 110, 126
Whitington 74
Wick, Richard de 66
Wildman 98
Wolf Rock 32, 45
Woodley 115, 127, 128, 131, 134
Worcester, William 73, 107

X

Xenophon 22

Z

Zidon 22